*d*ISCOVERING *a*USTRALIAN *w*INE

- a taster's guide -

ENJOY WINE
  - with food
  - with others
  - with feeling
  and in moderation

This book aims to enhance knowledge, appreciation and enjoyment of Australian wine. It is dedicated to the grapegrowers and winemakers of Australia, without whom none of this would be possible.

First published in Australia in 1995 by
Patrick Iland Wine Promotions
PO Box 131, Campbelltown
South Australia 5074

National Library of Australia
Cataloguing-in-Publication data:

Iland, Patrick
Gago, Peter

Discovering Australian Wine - a taster's guide
Includes index.
ISBN 0 646 22238 4

1. Australian Wine 2. Winemaking 3. Title

Design:
Melanie Horsman and Patrick Iland

Computer design, layout and illustrations:
Melanie Horsman

Project co-ordinator:
Judith Iland

Publisher:
Patrick Iland Wine Promotions

Cover photography:
Front: Henschke's Lenswood Vineyard, South Australia.
Inside front: A Chardonnay vine in the vineyards of Heemskerk Winery, Tasmania.
Pumping over a red wine ferment at St Hallett Winery, South Australia.
Woodstock Winery and Coterie, South Australia.
Inside back: Australian wine and food.
Back: Wine corks.

Printed in Australia by
Kitchener Press Pty Ltd,
Adelaide, South Australia.

Acknowledgements

We acknowledge the assistance and advice of many friends and colleagues during the writing of this book. Many sectors of the Australian wine industry have helped in various ways. We particularly acknowledge the support of the following companies: BRL Hardy, Brown Brothers, Campbells, Domaine Chandon, Henschke, Katnook Estate, Leeuwin Estate, McWilliam's, Mildara Blass, Mitchelton, Mountadam, Orlando Wyndham, Petaluma, Richard Hamilton, Rosemount Estates, Southcorp, Tyrrell's and Yalumba.

Some of the graphics were originally prepared by Graeme Lavis for our previous book 'An Introduction to Wine'.

We thank Margaret Cargill for doing a splendid job of editing the text, and Melanie Horsman of Kitchener Press for her creative ideas and design.

*P*atrick **Iland** is a senior lecturer in viticulture in the Department of Horticulture, Viticulture and Oenology at The University of Adelaide, South Australia. Prior to 1991, he was a lecturer at Roseworthy Agricultural College (the first college of viticulture and oenology in Australia), which has amalgamated with The University of Adelaide. Patrick teaches and researches in viticulture (the science of grape-growing) and in grape and wine chemistry.

He is a past winner of The Vin de Champagne Award and one of the two inaugural winners of the Stephen Hickinbotham Memorial Trust Award, the latter for his research work on Pinot Noir grapes and the viticultural factors influencing their composition. In 1993 he was one of the three recipients of the Stephen Cole the Elder Award for Excellence in Teaching awarded by The University of Adelaide.

He has experienced vintages in Australia and France, and enjoys tasting wines from different regions. He believes it is important to appreciate the diversity of wine styles. Patrick has a strong interest in and commitment to wine education and the promotion of a greater understanding of the culture of wine.

*D*rawn to the wine industry after eight years of secondary school teaching (mathematics and chemistry) in Victoria, **Peter Gago** completed a degree in Applied Science (Oenology) at Roseworthy Agricultural College in 1989, graduating Dux of the Course.

After four years as a maker of sparkling wines for the Penfolds Wine Group (now Southcorp), he joined its red winemaking department. He now functions in an extended winemaking role across the Southcorp wineries.

An avid wine collector and taster, Peter is passionate about Australian and overseas wine. He believes it is essential for a winemaker to gain an intimate appreciation of wine style differences and an understanding of a wine's development with time. Above all else, he advocates that wine is to be shared and enjoyed.

Peter's breadth of winemaking and tasting experience provide him with excellent credentials to being the co-author of this educational text on Australian wine.

About The Authors

CONTENTS

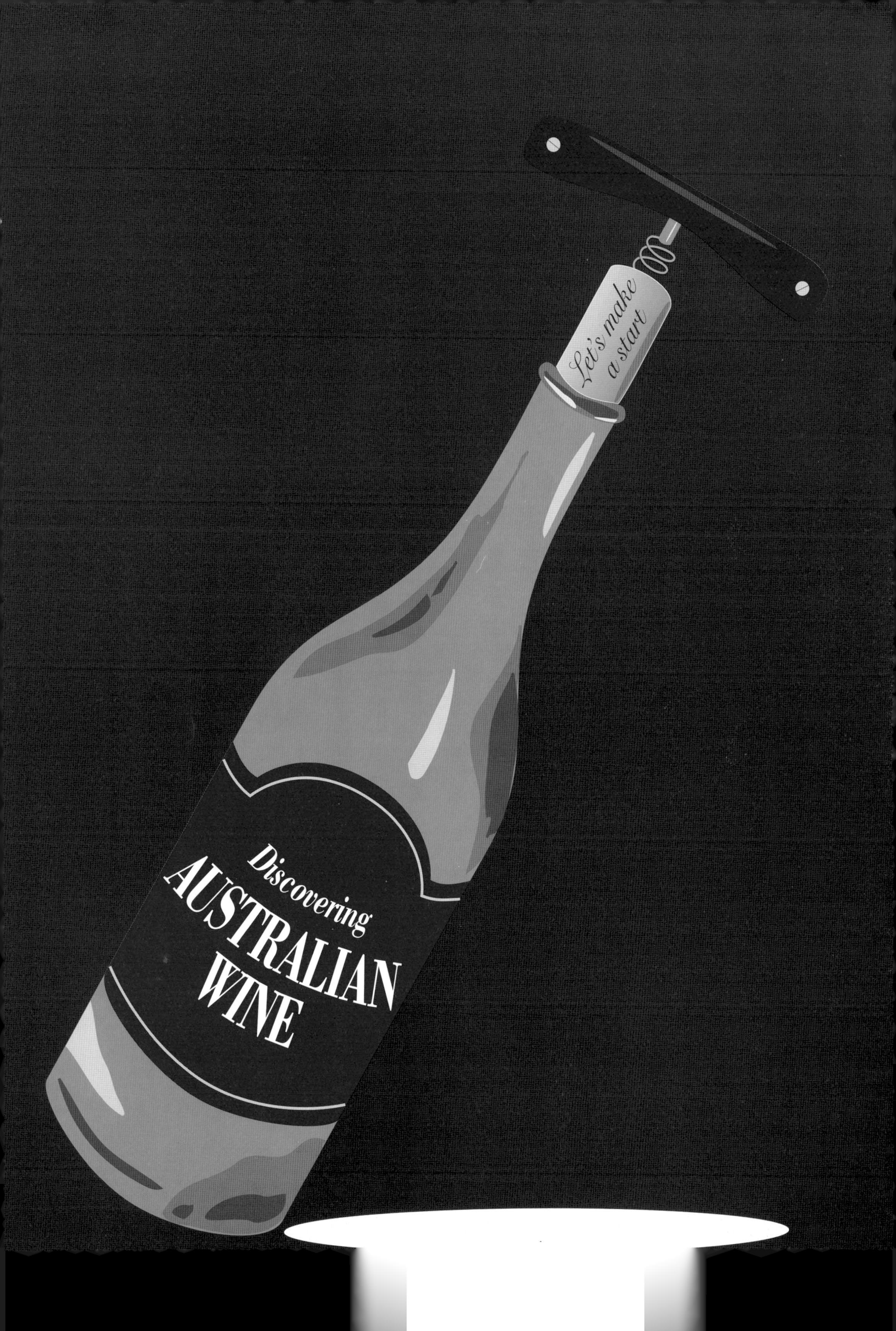
Let's make a start
Discovering
AUSTRALIAN
WINE

*T*he beginning of wine, about 7000 years ago, can be traced to sites in the Middle East. From there, the culture of the vine gradually spread to most parts of Europe, where wine has been made for about 2000 years. By comparison, Australians have been growing grapes and making wine for just over 200 years.

Vines were part of the cargo when the First Fleet arrived in Sydney in 1788, and were planted on land now the site of the Sydney Royal Botanic Gardens. From these beginnings in Sydney, the culture of the vine spread throughout Australia. By the 1890s, regions that we now know as the Hunter Valley, the Barossa Valley and the Yarra Valley were well established.

Before 1950 wine production in Australia focussed on fortified wines, but since then the emphasis has shifted steadily towards table wines. In the 1960s the sales of red table wine boomed, and a swing to white table wine followed in the 1980s. Red and white table wines are the major areas of production today.

European influence is everywhere in our wine industry. Many of our wine regions were developed by settlers of French and German ancestry. More recently, post World War II immigrants, also of European background, brought an ethos of wine to our country. Australians became aware and appreciative of the possibilities for enjoying wine with food and as part of their lifestyle.

Many wineries were established as family enterprises, their winemaking philosophy being passed down through the generations. The story of S. Smith & Son's Yalumba Winery in the Barossa Valley began in 1849 and now spans six generations; it is the oldest family owned winery in Australia.

The Tyrrell family have been producing wines in the Hunter Valley since 1858, maintaining a tradition which is now in its fourth generation.

The Tyrrell winemaking family - past, present and future.

In the Rutherglen area of Victoria, many winemaking families, including Chambers, Stanton and Killeen, Campbells, Morris and Bullers, have carried on the tradition of making Australia's most famous fortified wine - *Muscat of Rutherglen.*

You will find some of Australia's oldest living viticultural history in the vineyards of Chateau Tahbilk in Central Victoria. Vines were first planted here in 1860 and some vines growing today are now over a hundred years old.

The historic cellars of Chateau Tahbilk.

The historic clock tower of Yalumba Winery.

We can only speculate about whether the early vignerons could have imagined the Australian wine industry of today, an industry characterised by technological excellence, where innovative approaches in the vineyard and winery have revolutionised grapegrowing and wine production.

One of the major advances in wine production, particularly in making white wines, has been in the use of refrigeration throughout the winemaking process. Its widespread application in the Australian wine industry ensures that our wines are full of flavour, just like the grapes from which they were made.

But it is not just in the winery that changes have taken place; much has also happened in our vineyards. Australia has led the way in methods of pruning and harvesting grapes which lower the cost of producing wine. Many wine companies have research and development programmes aimed at improving the quality of grapes: studies on improved planting material, innovative trellis designs and irrigation scheduling, to name a few.

The last twenty years have seen great growth in the Australian wine industry, with the revival of many of the original sites (particularly in Victoria) and the discovery and establishment of many new areas as the culture of the vine spreads all around Australia. Most people will be familiar with regions such as the Hunter Valley, the Barossa Valley, Coonawarra and the Yarra Valley, but nowadays it may well be necessary to consult a map of Australia to find where some of our wines come from, areas such as Gumeracha, Bicheno, Manjimup, Tumbarumba, Lenswood and Murrumbateman.

The expansion of vineyard development into cooler climatic regions, by both large and small wine companies, has contributed to the quality image of Australian wine.

Approaches such as those taken by Brown Brothers of Milawa in north-eastern Victoria exemplify the willingness of the Australian wine industry to take on new ideas. John Francis Brown planted vines here in 1885 and crushed his first vintage in 1889. Subsequent generations have continued the tradition. The area is renowned for its fortified wines, a feature we take up later in the book, but the Brown family realised that the surrounding areas offered a range of climatic conditions for growing grapes.

Brown Brothers planted vines in a range of sites, and set about finding which grape varieties were best suited to each site. One of their vineyards is Whitlands, established in 1982; at 800 metres altitude (in the foothills of the Alps), it provides ideal conditions for growing aromatic white wine grape varieties such as Riesling and Gewürztraminer. Full flavoured red wines from varieties such as Shiraz come from vines grown in warmer, lower altitude sites.

As well as focussing on 'understanding the vineyard', they have built an experimental winery (called 'The Kindergarten Winery') where winemaking approaches are trialled before their adoption in the larger winery.

Brown Brothers' vineyard at Whitlands, in the King Valley, is one of Australia's more recent vineyard developments.

The Kindergarten Winery - cradle of Brown Brothers' future wines.

The fact that wineries can source grapes from a range of climatic sites is important in understanding the diversity of wine styles that are made by any winery. Large wine companies will source grapes from a number of regions, whereas smaller wineries will often make wines only from grapes grown in vineyards in close proximity to their winery.

The great choice of Australian wine is made possible by this diversity of vineyard sites, blending possibilities and a mix of large and small wineries in most of our winemaking regions.

$\mathcal{V}$ineyards are located in every Australian state and territory. The map below gives a guide to Australia's established and newer wine regions. Some are well known regions with famous reputations for their wines, while others are just being established. As well as new regions with new names appearing in the future, there may be changes in the naming and distribution of the boundaries of some of the established regions. Some regions are further divided into sub-regions. This is all part of the plan to define clearly the geographic locations of Australia's wine regions as Australia becomes a more significant part of the world wine scene. Australia is a large continent; the regions in which grapes grow cover a wide climatic spectrum and thus our winemakers produce many different types and styles of wine. The major wine producing regions are found in South Australia, Victoria and New South Wales.

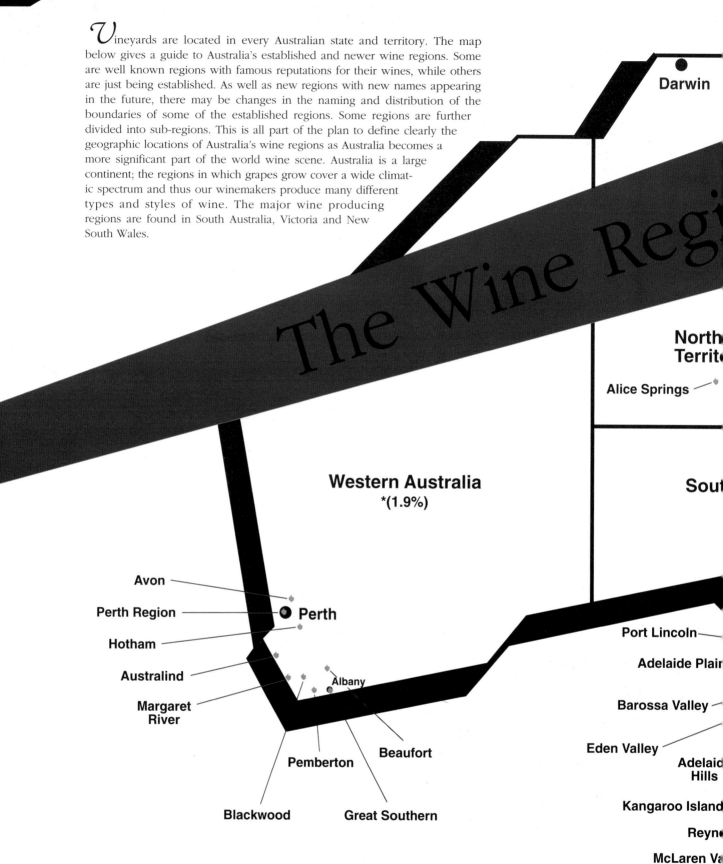

*The figures in brackets show each State's percentage of the total tonnes of grapes used for winemaking in Australia. (*Data from the Statistical Report of the Winemakers Federation of Australia Incorporated.*)

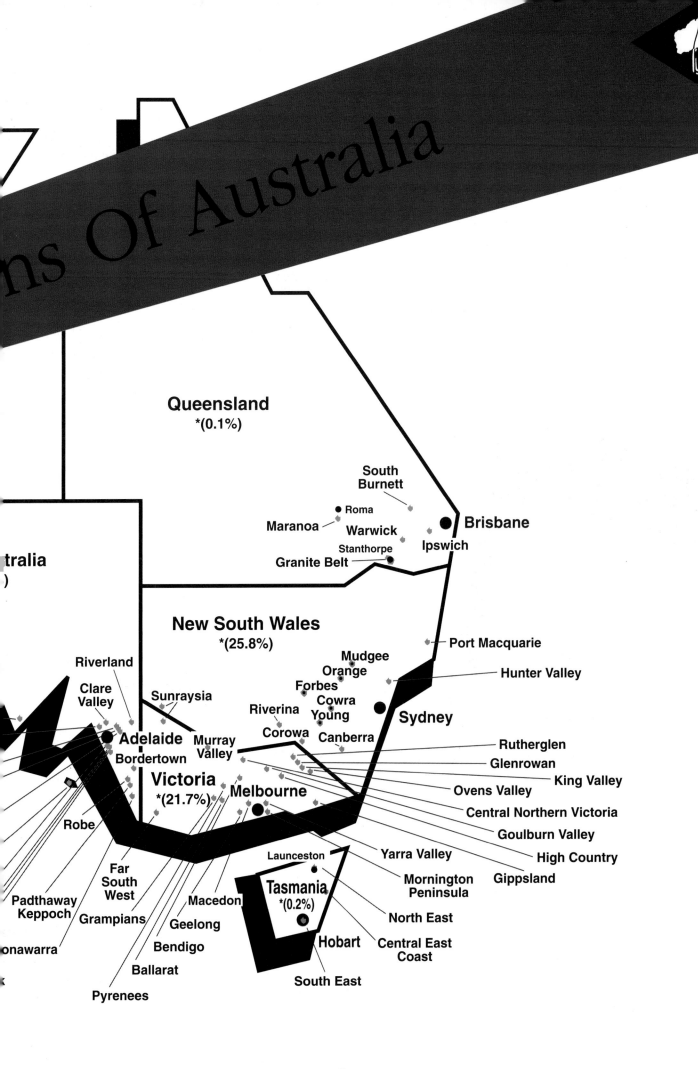

Queensland
*(0.1%)

South
Burnett

● Roma
Maranoa
Warwick
Stanthorpe
Granite Belt

● **Brisbane**
Ipswich

New South Wales
*(25.8%)

tralia
)

Riverland
Clare
Valley
Sunraysia

Mudgee
Orange
Forbes
Riverina
Cowra
Young
Corowa
Canberra

Port Macquarie

Hunter Valley

● **Sydney**

Rutherglen

● **Adelaide**
Bordertown

Murray
Valley

Victoria
*(21.7%)

● **Melbourne**

Robe

Far
South
West

Padthaway
Keppoch

Grampians

onawarra

Macedon

Geelong

Bendigo

Ballarat

Pyrenees

Launceston
●

Tasmania
*(0.2%)
◉

Yarra Valley

Mornington
Peninsula

North East

Hobart

Central East
Coast

South East

Glenrowan

King Valley

Ovens Valley

Central Northern Victoria

Goulburn Valley

High Country

Gippsland

GRAPES

to

WINE

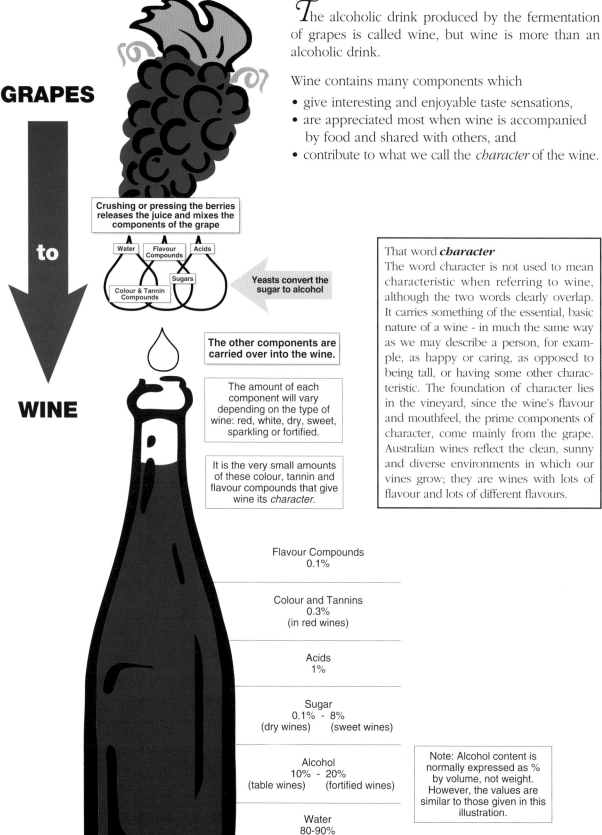

*T*he alcoholic drink produced by the fermentation of grapes is called wine, but wine is more than an alcoholic drink.

Wine contains many components which

- give interesting and enjoyable taste sensations,
- are appreciated most when wine is accompanied by food and shared with others, and
- contribute to what we call the *character* of the wine.

Crushing or pressing the berries releases the juice and mixes the components of the grape

Water | Flavour Compounds | Acids

Sugars

Colour & Tannin Compounds

Yeasts convert the sugar to alcohol

The other components are carried over into the wine.

The amount of each component will vary depending on the type of wine: red, white, dry, sweet, sparkling or fortified.

It is the very small amounts of these colour, tannin and flavour compounds that give wine its *character*.

That word **character**

The word character is not used to mean characteristic when referring to wine, although the two words clearly overlap. It carries something of the essential, basic nature of a wine - in much the same way as we may describe a person, for example, as happy or caring, as opposed to being tall, or having some other characteristic. The foundation of character lies in the vineyard, since the wine's flavour and mouthfeel, the prime components of character, come mainly from the grape. Australian wines reflect the clean, sunny and diverse environments in which our vines grow; they are wines with lots of flavour and lots of different flavours.

Flavour Compounds
0.1%

Colour and Tannins
0.3%
(in red wines)

Acids
1%

Sugar
0.1% - 8%
(dry wines)   (sweet wines)

Alcohol
10% - 20%
(table wines)   (fortified wines)

Note: Alcohol content is normally expressed as % by volume, not weight. However, the values are similar to those given in this illustration.

Water
80-90%

Some components of wine: approximate percentage composition (by weight)

1 Wine is made from grapes. White wines are made from white wine grape varieties (which are coloured various shades of green or yellow), and red wines from red wine grape varieties (which are coloured red, purple or black).

Some white wine grape varieties:

Chardonnay
Riesling
Sauvignon Blanc

Some red wine grape varieties:

Shiraz
Cabernet Sauvignon
Pinot Noir

2 Crushing the bunches breaks each berry into its parts and releases the juice. The mixture of juice, pulp, skins and seeds is called *must*.

To make white wine the must is pressed to separate the juice from the solids. Sometimes, the crushing operation is avoided and whole bunches are gently pressed to release the juice.

White wine is made from only the juice of grapes.

Red wine is made from the mixture of berry parts (the must) obtained after crushing bunches of black grapes. The colour of black grapes is contained in the skin of the berry and thus the skins need to be kept in contact with the juice to provide colour in the wine.

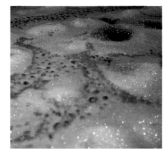

Red wine is made from the mixture of all berry components.

3 The sugars present in the liquid are then converted to alcohol by the action of yeasts. The yeasts are either naturally present on the skin of the berries or are added to the juice or must by the winemaker. This process, whereby the juice or must is converted to wine, is called *fermentation*. Other components of the grape (eg, acids, flavour and colour compounds) are also carried over into the wine. Some remain unchanged, while others are modified through winemaking techniques or by the passage of time.

The winemaker has to make decisions about how he/she will ferment and handle a particular batch of grapes.

What temperature?
Which yeast?
How long to leave the skins in contact with the fermenting liquid?
Whether to store the wine in oak barrels?
When to bottle?

4 The alcoholic drink produced by the fermentation process is called wine. Understand and respect wine's alcohol content and be moderate in its consumption.

Wine comes in many types and styles, but that is what adds to the fascination and enjoyment of wine.

Explore the following pages and discover the character of Australian wine.

How Wine Is Made - The Basics

Wine type

Variations in grape composition and winemaking technique lead to sensory differences in wines. We use the word *type* to distinguish between wines with large differences in their chemical make up: whether they are red or white, taste dry or sweet, contain bubbles of carbon dioxide, or have low or high alcohol content.

Dry White Table Wine   *Semi-sweet White Table Wine*   *Dry Red Table Wine*   *Sparkling Wine*   *Fortified Wine*

These represent different *types* of wine. Often the label will indicate the wine type.

Wine style

Wines grouped into particular types do not all taste the same; some will smell and taste distinctively of the grapes from which they were made, while others will be more influenced by the winemaking technique or by age. These (often more subtle) differences between wines of the same type are described as *style* variation. The words that describe style indicate whether the wine will be light, medium or full-bodied and what specific smell and taste sensations are evident at the time of tasting.

Australian wines come in a diversity of styles reflecting the climates and soils of our viticultural regions and the skills and personalities of our grapegrowers and winemakers.

Riesling   *Sauvignon Blanc*   *Chardonnay*

These represent wines of the same type (dry white table wine) but of different *styles*. The style will be different because they are made from different grape varieties. You have to taste the wine to assess what style it is; the label may give some clues.

Chardonnay 1   *Chardonnay 2*   *Chardonnay 3*

Even wines from the same variety may vary in style, depending on where the grapes were grown and how the wine was made.

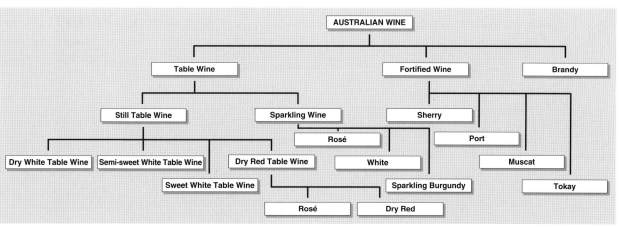

Australian wines can be classified into a number of wine types according to their chemical composition.

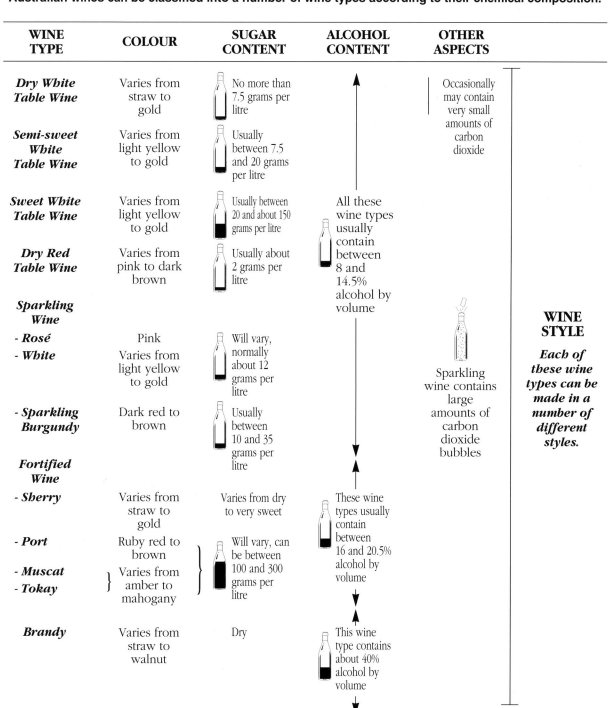

WINE TYPE	COLOUR	SUGAR CONTENT	ALCOHOL CONTENT	OTHER ASPECTS	WINE STYLE
Dry White Table Wine	Varies from straw to gold	No more than 7.5 grams per litre		Occasionally may contain very small amounts of carbon dioxide	
Semi-sweet White Table Wine	Varies from light yellow to gold	Usually between 7.5 and 20 grams per litre			
Sweet White Table Wine	Varies from light yellow to gold	Usually between 20 and about 150 grams per litre	All these wine types usually contain between 8 and 14.5% alcohol by volume		
Dry Red Table Wine	Varies from pink to dark brown	Usually about 2 grams per litre			
Sparkling Wine					**WINE STYLE**
- **Rosé**	Pink	Will vary, normally about 12 grams per litre			Each of these wine types can be made in a number of different styles.
- **White**	Varies from light yellow to gold				
- **Sparkling Burgundy**	Dark red to brown	Usually between 10 and 35 grams per litre		Sparkling wine contains large amounts of carbon dioxide bubbles	
Fortified Wine					
- **Sherry**	Varies from straw to gold	Varies from dry to very sweet	These wine types usually contain between 16 and 20.5% alcohol by volume		
- **Port**	Ruby red to brown	Will vary, can be between 100 and 300 grams per litre			
- **Muscat**	Varies from amber to mahogany				
- **Tokay**					
Brandy	Varies from straw to walnut	Dry	This wine type contains about 40% alcohol by volume		

The year in which the grapes were harvested. If a vintage year is shown 85% or more of the wine must be from the named vintage year.

A brand name, which may or may not be associated with the name of the producer.

The alcoholic content.

The alcoholic strength shown on the label will give you a guide to the alcohol content of the wine. For wine sold in Australia, the actual alcohol content can be ± 1.5% alc/vol of the stated level. This figure varies for other countries.

If a geographic area is shown, 85% or more of the product must come from that specific locality.

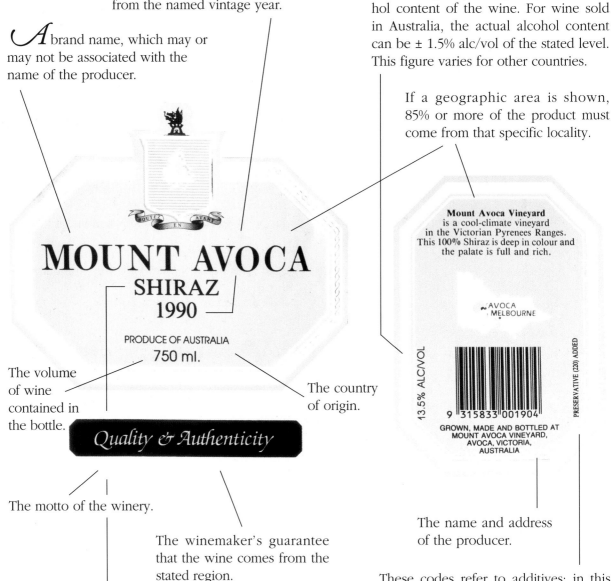

The volume of wine contained in the bottle.

The country of origin.

The motto of the winery.

The winemaker's guarantee that the wine comes from the stated region.

The name and address of the producer.

These codes refer to additives; in this case, 220 indicates that sulphur dioxide has been added to the wine during processing. We discuss the use of additives in the section on winemaking.

The variety/varieties from which the wine was made. (In this case the wine is 100% Shiraz.) If labelled as a single variety, a minimum of 85% of the product must be of the named variety. When the wine is made from a number of varieties, they are normally named in order of their contribution by volume. When the wine is blended from a number of varieties and/or regions it is most likely that it will not be labelled as a varietal wine.

Mount Avoca is one of the wineries in the Pyrenees region of western Victoria. Other wineries in the region are Chateau Remy, Summerfield, Mountain Creek, Taltarni, Warrenmang, Dalwhinnie and Redbank. The wineries of this region are well-known for the quality of their dry white and red table wines, and Chateau Remy and Taltarni Vineyards specialise in sparkling wine as well.

Varietal, descriptive and generic labels

Currently Australian wines can be labelled according to:

- **Varietal identification** - the grape variety/varieties from which it was made, for example, Riesling, Chardonnay, Marsanne, Pinot Noir, Shiraz, Cabernet Sauvignon.

- **Descriptive labelling** - where additional words are used to further describe the style. For example, sweet white wines can additionally have the words 'spätlese', 'late picked' or 'botrytis' on the label to indicate the degree of sweetness/style.
  Port can be labelled vintage, tawny, liqueur or ruby.

- **Generic classification** - relates to a style and is often named after the vinegrowing districts where the style originated. For example, Champagne indicates a sparkling wine style.
  Claret, Moselle, Sherry and Port are other generic names that you will be familiar with.

However, confusion arises because wines labelled in this manner may not necessarily be made from similar varieties or by similar methods to those of the region of origin. Thus, they do not truly represent the characters of that style. Words such as Champagne, Chablis, Burgundy, Moselle and Chianti should only be used for wines produced in those regions of Europe. These names were adopted by our early wine producers, many of whom were of European descent. However, the use of these names has always been a contentious issue, which has only recently been resolved by negotiations between the Australian Government and the European Community. The current agreement is detailed below. This agreement (part of The Bilateral Treaty for Trade in Wine between the European Economic Community (EEC) and Australia) provides for the phase out of use by Australian winemakers of the following terms:

by 31 December 1993	by 31 December 1997
- Beaujolais*	- Chianti
- Cava	- Frontignan
- Frascati	- Hock
- Sancerre	- Madeira
- Saint Emilion/St Emilion	- Malaga
- Vinho Verde/Vino Verde	
- White Bordeaux	

* except where agreements with individual producers provide otherwise.

At a date to be agreed by the parties having account of the commercial significance to both parties and the number of names used by Australia:

- Burgundy	- Chablis	- Champagne
- Claret	- Graves	- Marsala
- Moselle	- Port	- Sauternes
- Sherry	- White Burgundy	

In return the EEC have accepted the variation in grapegrowing and winemaking practices that are part of making wine in Australia. These concessions will further open up opportunities for Australian wine companies to export their wines to Europe, adding to our ever expanding export industry. Australian wines are now enjoyed in many parts of the world including New Zealand, Europe, the USA, the United Kingdom and Asia.

- **Wine show medals**

Various district and capital city agricultural societies run wine shows where wine companies can enter wines to be judged by a panel of expert judges. Wines are awarded points out of 20.

Wines are given awards as shown below:

Gold Medal 18.5 - 20.0 points
Silver Medal 17.0 - 18.4 points
Bronze Medal 15.5 - 16.9 points

As well as awards, trophies may be given to the best wines in particular classes.

These awards and trophies can then be displayed on the bottle.

If a wine consistently wins silver and/or gold medals at a number of wine shows, it is highly likely that it is a very good wine. Good wines will consistently score bronze medals. However, the absence of any wine show awards on a bottle of wine does not necessarily indicate failure at wine shows, as not all Australian wine companies enter their wines in these shows.

- *A*ustralian wine producers, unlike their European counterparts, grow a number of grape varieties in any particular region. Thus, you are likely to find Riesling, Chardonnay, Shiraz and Cabernet Sauvignon vines (and wines made from them) in most Australian wine regions. Each region will produce a different style of wine from each variety.

- Further, our winemakers are not obligated to produce wines according to regional traditions and/or regulations, as in some areas of Europe. Australian winemakers may make their wines by traditional methods, newer approaches, or perhaps a blend of both philosophies; it all depends on the style of wine they intend to produce.

- Freedom to source grapes from a range of areas and to blend wines from different varieties and/or regions offers the opportunity for wine companies:

  to increase and enhance their range of wine styles, and

  to produce larger volumes of popular 'brand' names of consistent quality.

Some of Australia's popular 'brand' names.

- Sometimes wine producers will blend wines from different regions to obtain a particular style, while at other times they will make wines exclusively from grapes grown in one region. Some regions have introduced a more detailed system to indicate the origin of the wine, eg, when a wine from the Mudgee Region carries the *appellation* mark (shown above) on the bottle, it is a guarantee that the wine was made at the vineyard from grapes grown on the property.

However, even though a region such as Mudgee may be well recognised for producing quality wines, these systems are only a guarantee of the origin of the wine and not a statement of any quality rating. The quality of any particular wine can only be assessed by tasting it.

The mark of the Society for the Appellation of the Wines of Mudgee (left) and the Tasmanian Appellation of Origin System (right).

- Many wine producers, irrespective of where they are based, may own vineyards in or source grapes from many grape growing regions of Australia. The grapes may be used to produce a wine that is labelled as a variety coming from a particular region, or as a blend of varieties with a region either declared or not, or as a 'brand' name.

The Rosemount Estate winery is located near Denman in the Upper Hunter Valley, but its wines are made from grapes which come from vineyards in many of the viticultural regions of Australia. Rosemount Estate, like many other Australian wine companies, produces a range of quality wines from different varieties and different regions.

• *M*any wine producers (both large and small) make a range of wines of varying styles, often under different labels.

Dromana Estate is a small, family owned vineyard on Victoria's Mornington Peninsula. As well as the Dromana Estate range of wines, which highlights the qualities of the Mornington Peninsula region, another label, known as Schinus, is also produced. Dromana Estate wines are produced from grapes grown in the Mornington Peninsula, while those under the Schinus Label may come as well from specially selected vineyards in areas as diverse as the Yarra and King Valleys in Victoria and Coonawarra and McLaren Vale in South Australia. The label on each bottle will indicate the source of the grapes.

A choice of wine styles from Dromana Estate.

• Many of the labels on Australian wine bottles feature the names of medium to large companies. These companies produce not only the large volume 'brand' names, but also premium wines which represent some of the best Australia has to offer.

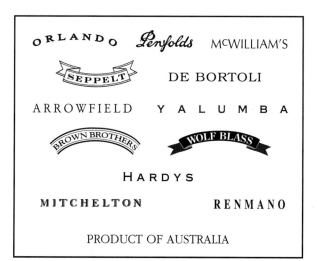

The names you will find on labels from some of Australia's medium to large wine companies.

• There are also hundreds of small wineries (often referred to as *boutique*) that form another significant part of the Australian wine industry. Most of these make their wines from grapes grown only in their own region and produce mainly premium varietal, regional wines, wines that not only express the character of the region but often the personality of their maker.

Labels from some of Australia's boutique wineries.

• **ENJOY WINE IN MODERATION**
Many bottles of Australian wine now carry this message to encourage people to take a sensible approach to drinking wine. The label may also indicate the number of standard drinks contained in the bottle.

THE WINE IN THE GLASS

The taste of it all

Wine - A Fascinating Drink

ine is a fascinating drink. Its tastes come not only from the grapes from which it was made, but also from the winemaking process and the changes that occur as the wine ages. For these reasons wine can have many different tastes. This book is about discovering the tastes of Australian Wines.

We will take you on a tasting journey through the many styles of Australian wine.

You will

- explore the diversity of tastes of wines made from Riesling, Chardonnay, Pinot Noir, Cabernet Sauvignon, Shiraz and other grape varieties;

- taste a piece of history at wineries such as Yeringberg in the Yarra Valley, Campbells of Rutherglen and Henschke of Eden Valley;

- experience the taste of wines from new vineyard developments, including Pipers Brook in Tasmania, Cowra in New South Wales and Margaret River in Western Australia; and

- indulge yourself with the taste of one of the world's greatest wines - Penfolds Grange.

Throughout the book we discuss the importance of what happens in the vineyard and the winery in shaping the taste of the wine. However, there will always be a part of wine that will remain a mystery, something that gives great wines their character. It is simply the completeness of these wines on the palate that make them so enjoyable; they epitomize the fascination of wine.

Taste wine wisely

It is generally agreed that drinking wine in moderation is beneficial to your health and lifestyle. However, it must always be remembered that different wines contain different amounts of alcohol. The effects of alcohol can vary from person to person for many reasons, including gender, individual body weight and metabolism. A sensible approach to tasting and drinking wine must always be advised. As a guide, the recommendation of The National Health and Medical Research Council is that *a sensible and moderate alcohol consumption, with reference to wine, is four standard drinks a day for men and two for women*.

What do we mean by a *standard drink?* It is the amount of wine that contains 10 grams of alcohol. Because different wine types contain different amounts of alcohol, the volume that is equivalent to a standard drink is different for each wine type.

The alcohol content of dry white, semi-sweet white, sweet white, sparkling and dry red table wine is between 10 and 14%v/v (alcohol by volume), and a standard drink is in the order of 120 ml.

For fortified wine, where the alcohol content is about 20%v/v, a standard drink is about 60 ml.

For brandy, where the alcohol content is about 40%v/v, a standard drink is about 30 ml.

Wine is most enjoyed when accompanied with food, and we have included some suggestions that will help you to match wine and food. Further, wine should be enjoyed in moderation. These issues, while covered only briefly in this book, are important if you are to appreciate wine for what it is - an enjoyable drink to be shared at the table with family and friends.

Talking about wine

To talk about wine is to share with others the experience of tasting different wines. We use words that describe different taste sensations and how they interact with each other. Other expressions convey the overall features that are present in particular styles of wines. Some examples of 'how we talk about wine' are shown here. We discuss these words and expressions, and many more, throughout the book.

Smooth, rich, luscious -a classic Muscat.

An interesting Semillon, vibrant grassy characters.

'The wine is pale lime green in colour. The nose and palate show citrus and grassy Semillon fruit characters. Medium-bodied, flavoursome palate balanced with crisp acidity.'

'Deep crimson red colour. A medium- to full-bodied wine with exceptional harmony between primary fruit, oak and aged characters. Minty, blackcurrant, dusty, smoky, cigar-box characters on the nose and palate. As well as the flavours, what I like about this wine is the feel of the tannins, that pleasing grainy sensation in the mouth.'

Discover the language of wine

Discover

- what we mean when we say a wine is, for example, *balanced, complex, astringent, well-structured....*
- some words to describe the smells and tastes of
  - different grape varieties
  - wine that has been stored in oak barrels, and
- why we use groups of words to describe different wine styles.

'A full-bodied Chardonnay with aromas and flavours of melon and peach-like fruit, combined with toasty, cheesy and nutty characters from barrel fermentation and oak storage. A rich, complex, flavoursome palate with a creamy texture and a lingering aftertaste.'

'A bouquet of raisins and toffee. Smooth, rich and luscious on the palate - a classic Muscat.'

*T*he term '*tasting wine*' is used here in a broad sense to describe the steps in assessing the colour and clarity, the smell and the taste on the palate of any particular wine.

1 SIGHT

2 SMELL

3 TASTE

Pour about 30 ml of wine into a glass.

 Sight

- Tilt the glass slightly.
- Check that the wine is clear (not hazy).
- Observe its colour against a white background and determine the depth (*intensity*) and shade (*hue*) of colour. Look at the rim and the body of the wine: the colours may be different. Are the colours brilliant, dull?
- Look for viscosity: if a wine is high in glycerol and/or alcohol, droplets of the wine may adhere to the side of the glass after the wine is swirled.
- Record the words that describe the wine's appearance.

Smell

Sniff the wine. Swirl the glass and then sniff the wine again. A couple of sniffs are sufficient as our sense of smell is easily fatigued and when this happens it becomes more difficult to detect and discern the odours.

- Check if the wine is clean, ie, does not have any mouldy, acetic (vinegar-like) or dirty (smelly) characters.
- Attempt to recognise and describe the various smells. These fall into three possible categories:

Sparkling wine is best enjoyed in a tall narrow glass, eg, a flute.

Check the colour of the rim

and the body of the wine.

The International Standards Organisation (ISO) glass, a suitable glass for tasting most types of wine.

We discuss the types of colours, smells and tastes that you find in different wines in the section on wine styles.

primary fruit characters	*and/or*	**developed (secondary) fruit characters**	*and/or*	**characters derived from the winemaking process**
		associated with the grape variety/varieties from which the wine is made		

The words that we use to describe smells (as well as flavours) are referred to as *descriptors*, eg, fruity, floral, raspberry, toasty, smoky. Often they are terms that you are familiar with from other sensory experiences.

- Estimate the *intensity* of these smell sensations: are they light, moderate or intense?
- Assess the *harmony* of the various sensations: no one smell, with the possible exception of fruit characters, should dominate.
- Record your impressions.

Describing smells can be difficult and you may need to do some training. There are many everyday situations which provide an opportunity to fine-tune your sense of smell and discover new descriptors. Experience the smells of the kitchen (the bread, spices, jams, honey, etc.) Explore the garden and take in its scents (the earth, grasses, flowers, vegetables, herbs, etc.)

Taste wines with groups of people, discuss and compare the smells you experience. Often when a particular descriptor is mentioned you can then recognise it in the wine. Everyone will not always agree on these terms and it is important that you use words that are meaningful to you. These then act as individual memory guides to that wine, or help to describe the particular style of the wine.

Some terms used when smelling wine

The nose: the overall smell sensations of a wine.

Aroma: the distinctive smell of the wine that is derived from compounds present in the grape at harvest - termed *varietal* or *primary fruit characters*. Each variety of grape imparts its own distinctive character to the wine, eg, citrus, floral, minty, herbaceous, blackcurrant. Characters that are not distinctive but give wine-like impressions are described as *vinous*.

Bouquet: those smells that evolve in the wine via the winemaking process and with time. As the wine matures, the distinct *varietal characters* are modified and now convey new sensations, termed *developed (secondary) fruit characters*, eg, the chocolatey, gamey or earthy odours that are obvious in some aged red wines. These developed characters are associated with the grape variety/varieties from which the wine was made. As well as changing with time, they integrate with any other characters that are derived from the winemaking process. This mixing and modification of characters starts during fermentation and continues while the wine is stored in the cellar and then in the bottle, this last stage being referred to as *bottle age*.

Throughout this maturation the bouquet grows in complexity and the aroma sensations become less obvious.

Descriptive terms/words

People associate certain images with particular experiences. A raspberry smells and tastes like a raspberry, a pineapple like a pineapple, etc. Similarly, Chardonnay grapes smell and taste like Chardonnay grapes. However, we often have less experience with the smell and taste of grape varieties and how they change from year to year and from vineyard to vineyard. Grapes develop characters recognised in other fruits, vegetables, etc, and it is often useful to describe grape varieties and wines with familiar terms such as raspberry, plums, citrus or licorice. These terms help us to communicate when tasting wines, to describe the aroma, bouquet and flavour (of wines).

These terms should be used in conjunction with words like 'is', 'smells like' or 'tastes like', as appropriate.

Some of the terms used may need to be imagined and others may not be grammatically correct, but they are nevertheless the commonly used terms, and provide a basis for communication.

3 Taste

Take a small volume of wine (about 10 ml) into your mouth. Move the wine around in the mouth for about 10-15 seconds. While the wine is in the mouth, think about its taste sensations. Then swallow or spit out the wine.

Have you ever wondered why wine tasters make those peculiar noises when tasting wine? It actually helps to get the most out of the wine. The warm environment of the mouth releases the volatile compounds from the wine, which then pass through the retronasal passage to the olfactory bulb in the nose. You are actually smelling the wine while it is in the mouth. Opening the mouth slightly and drawing air in help to aspirate the aroma and bouquet compounds out of the wine. This action, although a bit noisy, does enhance the perception of the wine's odour.

There are four basic tastes: *sweet, sour, bitter* and *salty.* We normally encounter only the first three when tasting wine. Detection of these tastes does not take place exclusively in any particular region of the tongue and it is important to move the wine around your mouth and over all parts of the tongue to fully appreciate them. *Bitterness* is the most localised of the taste sensations and its perception is concentrated towards the back of the tongue. The presence of bitterness can lessen the enjoyment of the wine.

Some exercises to familiarise yourself with these basic tastes:

Take a small portion of each of the solutions below into your mouth separately, move it over your tongue and experience the taste.

sweet	**sour (acid)**
mix a teaspoon of sugar into a cup of water.	squeeze a lemon into a cup of water, mix.

bitter
mix 2 teaspoons of
instant coffee into
a cup of warm water.
or
taste some tonic water which
contains quinine.

The compounds that give wine its aroma and bouquet also contribute to flavour sensations experienced in the mouth. These are sensed all over the tongue. Similar descriptors are used to describe flavour as are used for aroma and bouquet. Flavour sensations are also described as being light, medium or intense. Some sensations are more obvious immediately the wine enters the mouth, while others intensify as the wine warms up. The ever-changing nature of these flavour experiences is often referred to as the development or evolution of the wine in the mouth.

Another commonly used term is *complexity.* It describes the diversity of the odour and flavour sensations. We also use the terms length and aftertaste when referring to the flavour attributes of a wine; these relate to the intensity of flavour over the palate and how long the flavour sensations last in the mouth after the wine is tasted.

Astringent sensations (puckering of the mouth) are often experienced when tasting red wines, especially those high in tannins. The tannins interact with the saliva in the mouth, nullifying its lubricating action, and thus the mouth feels dry (as with a lack of saliva). Tannins can also contribute textures; tannins in red wines can feel soft, supple, firm, furry, grainy, dry and/or astringent in the mouth.

Textural features are not exclusive to red wines. White wines, particularly those that have been stored on yeast lees, can have a creamy feeling in the mouth. Another tactile sensation is that due to high or unbalanced alcohol levels present in some wines. These wines (either red or white) will give a warm or hot feeling at the back of the mouth, particularly after the wine has been swallowed.

All these tasting terms are described in the following pages.

$\mathcal{S}$ome wine tasting terms are easily understood, whereas others are somewhat more difficult to explain. *Body* is one of these more difficult concepts. Wines are described as being light-bodied, medium-bodied or full-bodied; these terms help to express the weight of the wine (how 'heavy' the wine feels) in the mouth. Body results from the combined effect of many of the wine's components but especially the amount of flavour, phenolics (tannins), sugar, glycerol and alcohol present in the wine. Essentially a dry, lower alcohol wine (eg, about 10% v/v) with medium flavour intensity will fall into the light- to medium-bodied category, whereas a wine with lots of flavour and tannins and higher alcohol (eg, about 13% v/v) will be classified as full-bodied. There are no definitive rules since wines will differ in their make up and different components may be responsible for the expression of body in any one wine. Wines lacking in body can tend to taste watery (*thin*). Alcohol is one of the more important contributors to the impression of body, and generally wines higher in alcohol content are more full-bodied. However, wines very high in alcohol and low in flavour will be unbalanced, in that the alcohol sensation will dominate the other features of the wine. Wine has many facets and *'getting the balance right'* is part of the art of winemaking.

> Although the nose of the wine may build our expectations, it is only when the wine is in the mouth that the full coming together of all the sensations is experienced - tastes, smells and flavours - their intensity, development and balance - the richness, feel and structure of the wine.

Experience the wine on the palate and look for

- the type, intensity and harmony of the sensory characters
- the weight of the wine in the mouth
- the balance between the acid and sweet tastes
- the balance between fruit characters and those of, for example, acid, sugar, alcohol, tannins, wood
- richness and fullness on the palate
- pleasant mouthfeel (tactile sensations)
- overall structure
- contribution of negative characters (eg, bitterness, coarseness, hotness, dirty or unpleasant odours, tastes or taints). These normally should not be present, but if they are, they should be minimal. Quality wines do not have to be squeaky-clean. It is the overall impression of the wine's positive features that portrays its quality, providing negative characters are not dominant.
- the length
- the finish.

Savour the experience: What are the features of the wine? Did you enjoy the wine?

If you are tasting a wine during a meal, or over a period of time, the characters of the wine may change as some air is absorbed into the wine in the glass. It is interesting to see how the wine develops and how it matches the food.

Some terms used when tasting wines

The palate: the overall flavour and tactile sensations on the tongue and mouth.

Sweetness: a sweet taste sensation due mainly to the sugar content of the wine. Sweet impressions unrelated to the sugar content can also be perceived; flavour compounds derived from ripe fruit and associated levels of alcohol and glycerol present in the wine can give an apparent sweetness on the palate. Sweet sensations are experienced all over the tongue.

Acidity: a crisp, refreshing taste sensation from the natural acids present in the wine. High levels of acid can have a drying effect in the mouth. (The concept of acidity is discussed further in the vineyard and winemaking sections.)

Freshness: a sensation. A wine that portrays freshness will not only be crisp, but will also have associated stimulating and fresh (not dulled with time) fruit aromas and flavours. Freshness is a quality that is derived from the grapes, and needs to be preserved throughout the winemaking process.

Astringency: a puckering (drying out) sensation over the mouth due to the reaction of tannins with the saliva in the mouth. This gives wine its grip and firmness. Tannins are derived from the grape and from the wood of oak casks. Astringency is more common in red wines.

Hotness: a warming, heated, sometimes almost burning sensation in the back of the mouth due to a high or unbalanced level of alcohol.

Tactile: a 'tangible' or 'feel' effect on the mouth, tongue and lips when wine is tasted. Sensations other than taste and smell become apparent. For example, tannin may have an astringent, drying (or 'chewy'!) effect. Oak may have a powdery, sometimes gritty effect. Alcohol may provide a hot or burning sensation.

Weight: a measure of a wine's mouthfeel that incorporates not only flavour intensity, but also other compounded effects derived from residual sugar, alcohol and oak.

Attack: the effect of the wine on the palate immediately it enters the mouth: whether it is smooth, soft, acidic, hard, aggressive. Notice, for example, the effect of the flavour impact, acids, tannins, oak and alcohol.

Length: the degree to which the taste sensations stretch across the palate.

Finish: the final taste experience of the wine immediately it is swallowed. Some words used to describe the finish of a wine would include: rich, alcoholic, hot, bitter, watery, abrupt, short, sharp, long, crisp, acidic, dull, flat, cloying, sour, clean, dirty, tannic, phenolic and oaky.

Aftertaste: desirable flavour sensations which linger in the mouth after the wine is swallowed. Aftertaste follows the finish. A wine is described as having a long, persistent or lingering aftertaste when the flavour sensations linger in the mouth for about 20 seconds or longer.

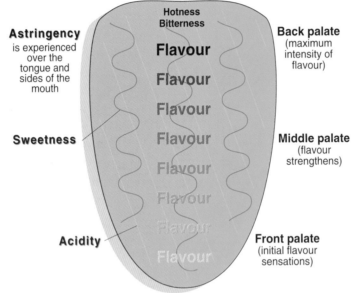

Diagram of a tongue

This diagram highlights the particularly sensitive areas for some tastes; however, most are experienced all over the tongue. Moving the wine around your mouth helps you discover everything that the wine has to offer.

*F*lavour: distinctive taste sensations that originate from compounds also responsible for the aroma and bouquet of the wine.

There are two types of fruit flavours:
i) primary fruit flavours
    (often termed *varietal character*); and
ii) developed (secondary) fruit characters
    (still characteristic of the variety).

Each variety of grape imparts its own distinctive flavour characters to the wine. Primary fruit flavours are derived from compounds present in the grape at harvest. These gradually change with time into other flavour compounds, which give different sensations. We call these developed or secondary fruit characters.

Other flavours come from winemaking practices, eg, from the oak during storage in oak barrels. Wine flavours, like aromas, change with time. At the stage of drinking, individual flavours should be distinct yet in harmony with each other. No one flavour, with the possible exception of fruit characters, should dominate. Flavour is experienced all over the tongue.

Synergy: the combination of separate flavours to produce a new flavour sensation, quite different from the individual components. It also applies to the combination of structural features. Although present in all wines, the effects of synergy are most obvious when winemakers blend wines.

Balance: the combined effects of the different flavour and structural components of the wine. When the wine is ready for drinking all the wine components should blend to convey harmonious smell and taste sensations, without any particular character dominating. The examples below attempt to explain these interactions. It is important to realise that it is the sum total of many diverse effects that convey the impression of a well-balanced wine. Balance changes with time, as the wine ages.

Acid-sweetness balance
A wine too high in acidity tastes sour and harsh and often displays unripe characters, whereas a wine high in sugar may taste sickly sweet or cloying. These sensations become apparent when the wine is out of balance. Attaining balance requires adjustment of either the acid or sugar level to nullify the excessive expression of the other. A well-made sweet wine, although very high in sugar content, can still taste refreshing and finish with apparent dryness if it is balanced by good acidity and/or phenolics from ageing in wood.

Acidity is also balanced by the sweetish impression of the alcohol and/or glycerol present in the wine.

Other balances
Primary and/or developed fruit character must also be in balance with each of the acid, sugar, alcohol, tannin and wood components.

Wine must be flavoursome. The quality and quantity of the fruit sensations (primary and/or developed) must be easily recognisable, while integrating with the array of other components.

These fruit profiles or images bring flavour, richness and interest to the palate. They should not be masked by excessive levels of other wine components.

The flavours of wine come from

the vineyard   *the winery*   *and time.*

Faults

Sometimes during the winemaking process smells and flavours will evolve (eg, due to oxidation or spoilage) that give the wine an unpleasant character. When these characters are present in excessive amounts the wine is said to be faulty.

Bitterness: a bitter (unpleasant) sensation on the back of the tongue and mouth, due to certain types of compounds such as phenolics in the wine.

Volatility: the smell of vinegar (acetic acid) and/or nail polish remover (ethyl acetate) in a wine. In small amounts it can contribute to complexity, but when present in large amounts it is regarded as a fault. Certain yeasts can produce these compounds or they can be present as a result of oxidation, a concept we discuss in the section on winemaking.

Aldehyde: the smell that you find in sherry style wines. In these wines it is a positive feature, but in table wines it is generally considered a fault, as it detracts from the fruit characters of the wine. It appears as a result of oxidation.

Hydrogen sulphide: the smell of rotten eggs, not a very pleasant odour to find in wines. It is produced by yeast, but does not persist very often in modern winemaking practices. Other related unpleasant odours that are sometimes present in wines can be described as garlic, onion and cabbage.

Corked: a mouldy and/or wet hessian bag type of smell, which can come from a contaminated cork. Cork is a natural product and sometimes it can contain moulds. These moulds react with some of the chemicals used during the production of corks to produce a compound which remains in the cork. When the cork is inserted in the bottle and then comes in contact with the wine, the contaminating compound diffuses into the wine and gives it a mouldy smell and taste. The wine is then said to be corked. Apart from this mouldiness, the aroma and flavour of the wine is masked. The contamination of the wine by this corked character can spoil an otherwise good wine.

Richness: an enhanced intensity of sumptuous aromas, bouquet and flavour tones, coupled with enjoyable fullness on the palate. Rich wines do not have to be sweet wines, or full-bodied wines. Richness is associated with grapes that really get ripe, ie, both sugar and flavour ripe: grapes from good vineyards and good years. It is associated with both primary and secondary fruit characters.

Smoothness/Softness: a pleasing all-over mouthfeel sensation, displaying no unbalanced, harsh or aggressive impressions. It also relates to the finish on the back palate. Glycerol contributes to the smoothness of a wine, increasing the viscosity (the thickness of the texture).

Roundness: a sensation that appears to fill the mouth all over, apparent in wines with good flavour and structure. Often used when describing Pinot Noir wines.

Tightness: a highly defined balance of structure, weight and flavour (often intense) on the palate.

Finesse and elegance: terms used to describe well-structured wines exhibiting delicate characters with all the desired features of the style present in perfect balance.

Complexity: a wine is described as complex when it provides a diversity of desirable smell and taste sensations in harmony with each other.

Complexity is derived from the various combinations of:
- primary fruit flavours
- developed fruit flavours
- winemaking contributed flavours.

Sometimes terms like *layers of flavours* and *layered* are used to describe a complex wine.

Structure: a difficult concept to explain. A wine is said to be well structured or to have good structure when the flavour properties (type, intensity, persistency) fit well with the tactile qualities of the wine. All the parts of the wine are integrated and complement each other. The overall taste just feels right. Good structure indicates a propensity to age (*longevity*). It incorporates the inter-relationship between many of the terms (flavour, balance, freshness, etc) described in this section.

**WINE IS MADE
UP OF MANY
COMPONENTS**

**ALL COMPONENTS
SHOULD BLEND
TOGETHER**

**TO STRUCTURE A
PARTICULAR TYPE AND
STYLE OF WINE**

*T*asting wine - putting it all together

Many sensations combine to produce the taste of any wine. Although we often tend to describe a wine by its parts, it is the coming together of these parts that makes the wine. The types and intensity of aromas and flavours, the complexity, balance, finesse, structure and mouthfeel, and their interrelationships, are what really indicate the quality of the wine - just like the pieces of a jigsaw fusing together to reveal the finished picture.

A check list:

Are the aromas and bouquet distinct, intense and complex? How would you describe them? Are there any off smells?

Are the flavours distinct, intense and complex?

How would you describe them?

What about the balance: is the wine too acidic? too sweet? Is there good balance between the fruit characters and those of, for example, acid, sugar, alcohol, tannin and oak?

Is the wine showing freshness and/or richness and/or roundness on the palate?

Does it have good mouth-feel?

For red wines, what is the 'feel' of the tannins?

Is it well-structured?

Are any negative characters dominating the palate?

How does the wine finish?

Is the aftertaste short or long?

Is the wine interesting and enjoyable?

Although it is not necessary to describe or record your impressions of the wine to fully enjoy its sensory experience, a few words about its flavour, balance, weight, mouthfeel, structure and interest can readily convey your impressions of the wine to other tasters. The occasion and the wine will often dictate how little or how much you need to say. Simply expressing your appreciation of the quality and interest of the wine may be all that is necessary, especially when it is accompanied by food and shared with friends, and when it adds to the overall enjoyment of the occasion. **The enjoyment of drinking the wine is, after all, what it is all about.**

*What to look for in a good wine?
It all depends on the style of the wine.
We talk about this in the section
on wine styles.*

The welcome sign to Katnook Estate, Coonawarra, South Australia.

Richmond Grove Barossa Winery: a premier Barossa Valley tasting facility on the banks of the Para River in Tanunda, South Australia.

Trentham Estate: a cellar door sales and restaurant complex on the banks of the Murray River near Mildura.

A warm welcome to taste the wines of Australia.
*M*any wineries have cellar door sales facilities, where you can taste their range of wines.

Plantagenet Wines: in a natural bush setting in the Great Southern region of Western Australia.

Choosing wine at Chapel Hill Winery, McLaren Vale, South Australia.

Take a guided tour of the cellars at Mitchelton Wines, in the Goulburn Valley of Central Victoria.

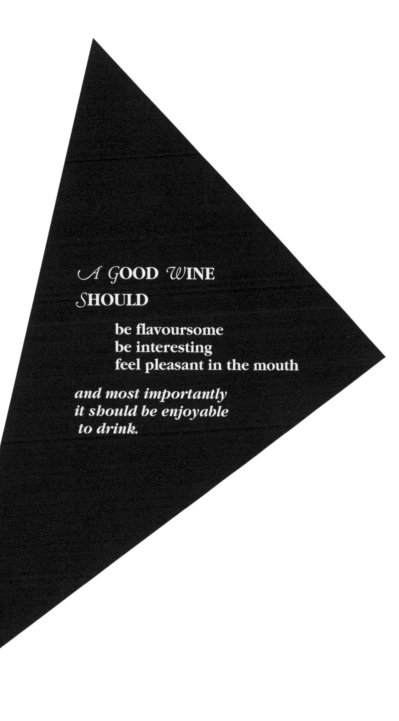

A GOOD WINE SHOULD

be flavoursome
be interesting
feel pleasant in the mouth

*and most importantly
it should be enjoyable
to drink.*

Vintage time at Leeuwin Estate Vineyards, Margaret River.

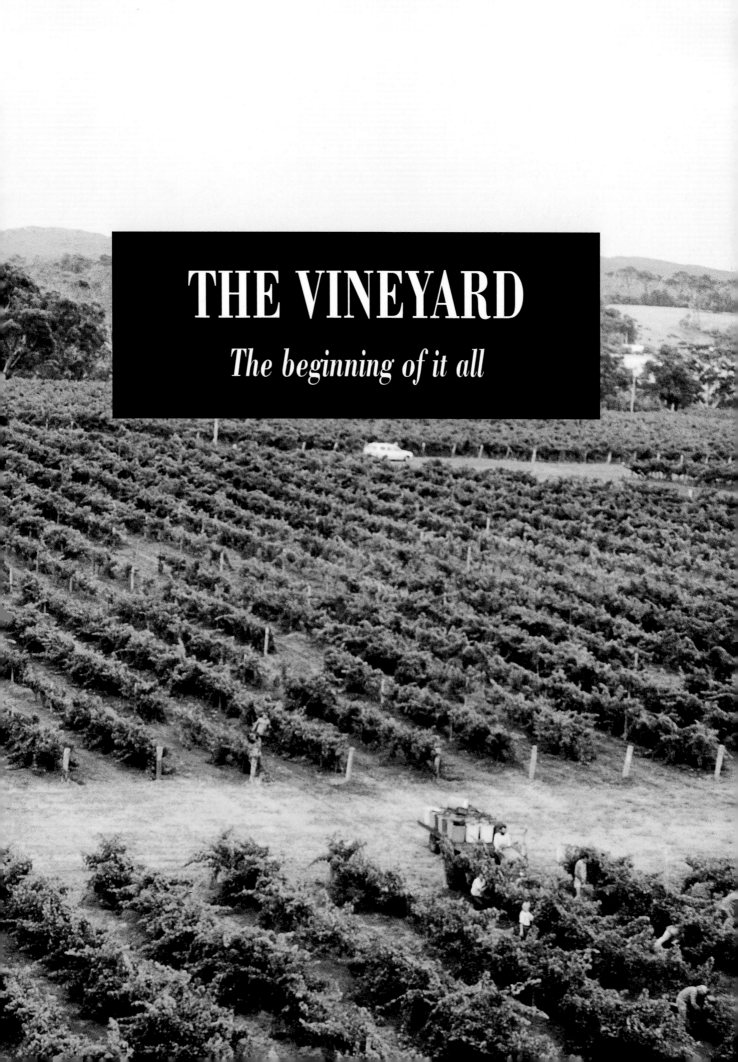

THE VINEYARD

The beginning of it all

The culture of the vine is spread over many parts of Australia. Some areas are already famous for their wines: Coonawarra, the Barossa Valley, the Hunter Valley, the Yarra Valley, to name a few. However the expansion of the wine industry into new vinegrowing regions is bringing other sites to prominence, names such as Pipers Brook in Tasmania, Margaret River in Western Australia, Cowra in New South Wales, Mornington Peninsula in Victoria and the Adelaide Hills in South Australia. These and many other regions are emerging as quality wine producing areas.

At any site the complex interactions between variety, climate, soil and vineyard practices control the growth of the vine, its performance and the composition of its grapes. Grapes will develop and ripen differently in different vineyards and it follows that the wines from each vineyard will also be different since many of the wine's sensory characters come from the grapes. Australian vineyards span a wide range of climatic environments, are planted on an assortment of soils and are managed in different ways. You should not be surprised then to discover that there is a range of wine types produced in Australia and that these come in many styles, the diversity of our vineyards being portrayed in the diversity of our wines.

It is not easy to describe why grapes from one vineyard are different to those of another, as there are so many contributing factors; grape variety, the climate and its variability, soil type and management practices associated with each site are some of the things we need to consider. They all form part of the big picture where the work of the grapegrower complements the influence of the natural environment in producing grapes for the many styles of Australian wine. Sugar, acid, colour, aroma and flavour compounds (and varying levels of these that are specific to the site) are formed in the grapes, and these largely determine the wine style coming from that vineyard.

Typically, Australian wines are full of flavour. They are made from grapes that come from well managed vineyards in sunny, non-polluted environments; such conditions ensure clean, flavoursome grapes from which our winemakers can begin to craft their wines.

Grapevine varieties

Wine grape varieties

Grapevines come in many shapes and forms. The vines that you see in Australian vineyards belong to the *species* referred to as *Vitis vinifera*. This species, which has its origins in the Middle East and Europe, has about 5000 different types, called *varieties*.

There are about 60 varieties in Australia, although most wine drinkers will be familiar with only twenty or so, names such as Riesling, Chardonnay, Semillon, Sauvignon Blanc, Pinot Noir, Cabernet Sauvignon and Shiraz. But we also grow many varieties that you do not often see on wine labels, such as Palomino and Pedro Ximenes, which are used for making sherry, and Pinot Meunier, a variety used in sparkling wine production.

Some white-wine grape varieties
(grapes are coloured various shades
of yellow or green)

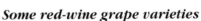

Chardonnay
Muscat Gordo Blanco
Riesling
Semillon
Chenin Blanc
Colombard
Crouchen
Sauvignon Blanc
Traminer (Gewürztraminer)
Frontignac
Marsanne
Sultana

Some red-wine grape varieties
(grapes are coloured various shades of red
and purple and are often referred to as
black grapes)

Cabernet Sauvignon
Grenache
Shiraz
Malbec
Merlot
Pinot Noir
Cabernet Franc
Ruby Cabernet
Touriga

Each variety has specific aroma and taste sensations, which we call varietal or primary fruit

characters. Some varieties have more distinctive characters than others, and it is these varieties that we commonly see on labels of varietal wines (wines made predominantly from a single variety).

Often wines from different grape varieties will be blended to produce a wine of more complexity, structure and interest.

Clones

Clones are sub-types within varieties. These sub-types differ in their genetic make up, or, as scientists put it, in the DNA structure of their cells. DNA is the component of living cells that gives each cell its genetic fingerprint and which governs every process and structure associated with that cell.

If over time some mutation occurs in the cell of a bud on a shoot on a particular vine and this shoot is taken as a cutting for planting in a new vineyard, the vine that arises from that cutting will be slightly different from all the other vines that have come from cuttings of unchanged vines. If there were many vines in the original vineyard that have undergone mutation, the new vineyard will now be a mixture of vines of the two clones (the original one and the mutated one). When this process occurs over many years, some vineyards may be made up of a number of different clones of the same variety. Therefore, differences may exist in the shape of the vines, in berry size, in berry colour and/or other features between vines in the same vineyard.

Varieties that have been used in winemaking for many years, such as Pinot Noir, have many clones, because there has been plenty of opportunity for mutation to occur in the vineyards. Other varieties, such as Ruby Cabernet, show less clonal variation since they are more recent and have had less opportunity to undergo changes.

Some clones seem to perform better than others under different environmental conditions. However, while there may be obvious differences between some clones, most mutations result in very slight differences and so-called clones will differ little in their performance in the vineyard.

Some winemakers prefer a specific clone for a certain style of wine and will select this clone when planting their vineyards, while others will choose to plant a selection of desirable clones, aiming for greater variability in the characters of the grapes coming from the vineyard and thus increasing the complexity of the resultant wine.

More recently, Australian grapegrowers have had greater access to the clones used in the vineyards of Europe. The future will be exciting as the search continues for the clones that are most suitable for our different grapegrowing regions. These improvements in planting material can only mean better quality grapes and wines.

Grapevine rootstocks

Vitis vinifera vines often do not perform well when planted on their own roots in soils with high lime or salt content and where pests such as *phylloxera* are present. In these circumstances it is best to plant grafted vines.

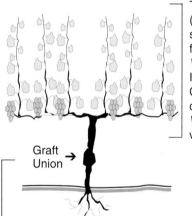

This part of the vine (upper wood, shoots, leaves and fruit) is from the *Vitis vinifera* variety. It could be Chardonnay, Shiraz or any of the many *Vitis vinifera* varieties.

Graft Union →

This part of the vine (the rootstock), which provides the roots, comes from another species (normally a native American species or a hybrid), which is resistant to attack by soil pests or grows well in certain soils.

Diagram of a grafted vine.

Grape phylloxera is a small aphid that lives on the roots (and sometimes leaves) of grapevines. This pest attacks the roots, which eventually decay, and the vine dies. In areas where phylloxera is present in the soil, *Vitis vinifera* vines must be grafted onto resistant rootstocks before they are planted. These grafted vines, now with a resistant and efficient root system, produce grapes of the selected *Vitis vinifera* varieties.

$\mathcal{P}$hylloxera is present in most countries. It destroyed the vineyards of Europe in the late 1800s and in more recent times it has ravaged vineyards in California. Phylloxera was found in Australia in the 1880s and destroyed many of the vineyards of Victoria during the late 1800s and early 1900s.

Effects of phylloxera on a vineyard.
The vines in the foreground are on own roots and have been attacked by phylloxera, while those in the background have been planted on resistant rootstocks and have survived.

The spread of phylloxera in Australia has been controlled by quarantine regulations that restrict the movement of grapevines between regions, and thus many Australian vinegrowing regions are not troubled by this pest.

Rootstocks are also used to combat nematodes, which are small worm-like organisms that live in some soils and disrupt root function, affecting the growth of the vine.

But rootstocks are used for other reasons than controlling soil pests; there are rootstocks that work better in salty soils and others that work better in soils of high lime content. Researchers are now looking for rootstocks that will decrease the vigorous growth that often occurs in vines growing in rich deep soils.

Over the years, grapevine breeders have conducted extensive research to find varieties suitable for the many different soil and environmental conditions in which the vine grows. The task of these researchers is not only to combat such pests as phylloxera, but also to breed varieties that are resistant to diseases that attack the grapevine.

Australia's vineyards of the future

The total annual production of grapes for wine is currently about 800,000 tonnes, coming from over 5000 independent grape growers and over 700 wine companies. This production will increase dramatically over the next ten years as vineyard development takes place to meet the ever increasing domestic and export demand for Australian wine.

New frontiers

Existing plantings are being redeveloped and new areas are being discovered and established. Australians have always had a readiness to try new ideas, and the developments that have emerged from our viticultural research are now being employed in the setting up of these sites. The vineyards will be planted with the best planting material (the best clones, the best rootstocks) coming from vine improvement programmes in each vinegrowing region. They will be trellised in innovative ways, irrigated with computer controlled technology and mostly machine pruned and harvested, such practices leading to cost effective production.

The extensive plantings, in a range of climatic sites, of premium varieties such as

Chardonnay	*Cabernet Sauvignon*
Shiraz	*Semillon*
Sauvignon Blanc	*Merlot*
Riesling	*Pinot Noir*

will ensure a plentiful supply and ample choice of quality Australian wines.

Continuing tradition

The life of a grapevine is usually about 40 years, and when vines reach this age the vineyard will be gradually replanted. However, we are lucky in Australia that some winemakers have chosen to maintain their vines way past this age. In the Barossa Valley and Ranges we can find Shiraz vines over 100 years old, vines which are producing uniquely full flavoured, full-bodied red wines. Two such vineyards are Henschke's Mount Edelstone vineyard and their Hill of Grace vineyard, both located close to the Henschke's winery at Keyneton in South Australia. The vines in Mount Edelstone are about 70 years old, while some of the old, low yielding vines in the Hill of Grace vineyard are about 130 years old. However as the vines grow old they start to die off and become less productive. A point is reached where sections of the vineyard require replanting.

Prue Henschke, their viticulturist, has the challenge of carrying out this redevelopment. She has devised a programme of meticulously assessing every vine in each vineyard for its growth and fruit quality characteristics and then selecting the best from which to take cuttings for the replanting.

By taking cuttings from these selected vines, nicknamed the 'super vines' (which represent a special pool of genetic material), the Henschke family hopes to maintain the character of each of these vineyards for future generations of wine consumers to enjoy. It is a laborious programme and the replanting could take another 50 years or more, but as Prue says, 'It is a labour of love, as some of these vines span five generations of the Henschke family. It is all about maintaining tradition.'

We will introduce you to these wines later in the book, as well as some other full-bodied Shiraz wines that come from the Barossa Valley, including Rockford's Basket Press Shiraz, St Hallett's Old Block Shiraz and Australia's most famous wine, Penfolds Grange.

Henschke's Hill of Grace Vineyard (Keyneton, South Australia) - Shiraz vines over a hundred years old.

*O*nce the vineyard is established, each vine grows according to an annual growth cycle. Temperature regulates the timing of each stage, and since temperature conditions vary from site to site the stages of vine growth occur at different times of the year in different vineyards. Each stage of growth occurs earlier in hotter regions than it does in cooler regions.

Temperature conditions also change from year to year. Hence, at any one site, the stages of vine growth will either be early or late depending on the conditions of that year.

Therefore grapes, either from different vineyards in any one year or from the same vineyard in different years, will ripen under different temperature and other climatic conditions.

These climatic differences, which influence how the grapes ripen, contribute to differences in wines produced from different vineyards (*the regional variation*) and from the same vineyard from year to year (*the vintage variation*).

However, many other factors also contribute to the sensory characters that develop in grapes, including variety, vineyard site, management practices and time of harvest.

The annual growth cycle of the grapevine

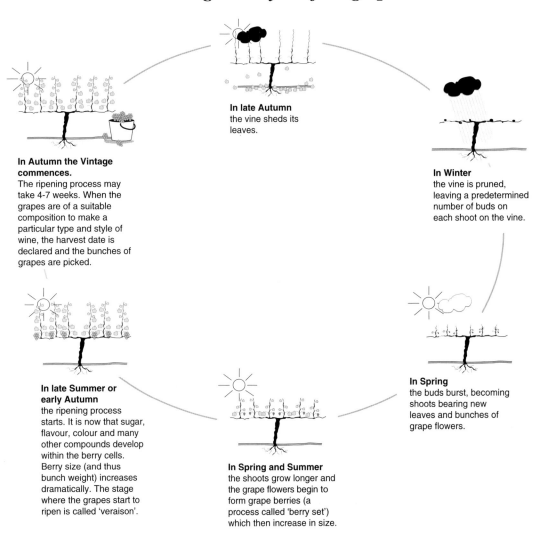

In late Autumn
the vine sheds its leaves.

In Autumn the Vintage commences.
The ripening process may take 4-7 weeks. When the grapes are of a suitable composition to make a particular type and style of wine, the harvest date is declared and the bunches of grapes are picked.

In Winter
the vine is pruned, leaving a predetermined number of buds on each shoot on the vine.

In late Summer or early Autumn
the ripening process starts. It is now that sugar, flavour, colour and many other compounds develop within the berry cells. Berry size (and thus bunch weight) increases dramatically. The stage where the grapes start to ripen is called 'veraison'.

In Spring and Summer
the shoots grow longer and the grape flowers begin to form grape berries (a process called 'berry set') which then increase in size.

In Spring
the buds burst, becoming shoots bearing new leaves and bunches of grape flowers.

An appreciation of wine begins with an understanding of vineyards.....

The sugar story

The main sugars in grapes are glucose and fructose

The leaves of the vine act like miniature chemical factories and produce sugar (a process called photosynthesis). The sugar is then moved through the shoot to other parts of the vine, including the developing berries. When the berries are small, hard and green (during the stage from berry set to veraison) this sugar is mainly used for berry growth and chemical reactions within berry cells. However, veraison signals the onset of ripening and now sugar begins to be stored in special compartments within the berry cells. From veraison to harvest the sugar content of the berries increases dramatically and berries become obviously sweet to taste.

Photosynthetic reactions occur in the leaves
(where carbon dioxide and water react to form sugar).

The energy for this reaction comes from sunlight.

ENERGY

SUGAR

The sugar produced in the leaves is moved through the shoot to the grape berries on each bunch.

WATER

The water comes from the soil via the roots.

Prior to harvest samples of berries are collected regularly from each vineyard and crushed to release the juice. The sugar content of the juice is measured and usually expressed in units of either °Baumé (degrees Baumé) or °Brix (degrees Brix). One °Baumé is equivalent to 1.8° Brix. °Baumé is more commonly used since it gives a convenient indication of the potential alcohol content of the wine produced from those grapes, eg:

- a grape juice with 10° Baumé (18° Brix) will, if fermented completely, produce a wine of about 10% alcohol by volume;

- a grape juice with 13° Baumé (about 23° Brix) will, if fermented completely, produce a wine of about 13% alcohol by volume.

Hence a measure of °Baumé taken prior to harvest gives the winemaker a guide as to the type of wine he/she could make from that batch of grapes, eg:

- sparkling wines are normally produced from grapes with sugar levels in the order of 9 to 11° Baumé;

- a full-bodied red wine requires grapes with a higher sugar level, about 13° Baumé;

- to make a muscat the grapes should be very high in sugar, sometimes up to 20° Baumé.

Apart from the increase in sugar in the berries during the ripening process, many other changes also occur. It is a period of great chemical activity within the berry. The berries soften, take up water, increase in size, decrease in acidity, change colour and develop distinctive aromas and flavours. While the sugar level at harvest essentially dictates wine type, it is the types, amounts and balance of these other components which are largely responsible for the style of any particular wine type.

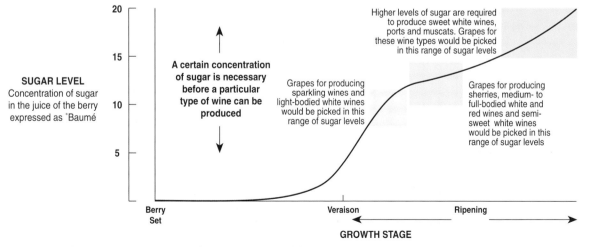

The relationship between the concentration of sugar in the juice of the berries at harvest and suitability to produce certain wine types.

35

Grapes - The Ripening Process

The acid story

The main acids in the grape are tartaric acid and malic acid

Acids are the components that give wine its fresh, crisp taste sensation. They originate in the grape but some may also be added during winemaking. Just as the sugar level is expressed by the term °Baumé, there are special terms that relate to the concept of acidity. The overall concentration of acid present in the juice of grape berries is expressed as titratable acidity, while the chemical effectiveness of the acids (how they influence chemical reactions in the juice) is referred to as pH. These terms are also used to describe acidity levels in wine and are often seen on wine labels. A more detailed coverage of acidity concepts is given in the section on winemaking.

Both tartaric and malic acids, which are produced in the berry during the early stages of berry growth, reach their maximum levels about veraison and then decrease in concentration during the ripening period. These changes are reflected in the measures of acidity; with berry ripening, titratable acidity decreases and pH increases.

Measurements of pH and titratable acidity are taken on the juice of the sample berries collected from each vineyard. The winemaker takes into consideration the values of these measurements and their balance with the sugar level in deciding when to pick the grapes.

The colour and tannin story

Colour and tannin compounds form part of the phenolic make up of wines. *Phenolics* are a group of chemical compounds that give wine its colour, influence its texture and palate weight and can contribute bitter and astringent (drying) taste sensations. Most of the phenolics are in the skins and seeds of the grape, and the compounds that give red wine its colour (the *anthocyanins*) are found only in the skins of black grapes. Peel a black grape and you will observe that the flesh is clear and only the skin is coloured black.

Veraison - the beginning of ripening and the time when the grapes start to change colour.

The onset of colouring in grapes is the most obvious change occurring at veraison. Berries of red-wine grape varieties change from green to red; this colour is modified during ripening as the anthocyanin content in the skin increases, and the berries take on a purple-black appearance. Colour changes in white-wine grape varieties, although less obvious, are also triggered at veraison, the dark green berries taking on either a lighter green or yellow appearance as ripening progresses.

The amount of colour in black grapes at harvest determines in part the colour of the wine made from them; lightly coloured grapes produce lightly coloured red wines while more intensely coloured grapes produce darker coloured wines.

The drying (puckering) sensation in the mouth, often experienced when tasting red wines, is associated with compounds called *tannins*. These have their beginnings in the skin and seeds of black grapes. As the berry ripens the tannin level in the skin generally increases, but as well as this the tannins that are formed are continually changing their structure. Both the amount and types of tannins in the grapes at harvest influence the mouthfeel of the resultant wine.

A black grape with and without its skin.

The aroma and flavour story

The aroma and flavour compounds which are present in the juice and skin of the berry are responsible for the distinctive aroma and flavour sensations of wines made from those grapes. These aroma and flavour sensations are often referred to as primary fruit or varietal character. As the berry ripens, there are changes in the types of characters expressed and an increase in the overall level of aroma and flavour compounds, albeit only in minute amounts. For example, with Pinot Noir grapes from some vineyards the juice from the berries may exhibit aroma and taste characters similar at first to strawberries, then raspberries and then plums.

Each variety of grape has its own set of varietal characters and its own pattern in which these change during ripening; we refer to this as the *primary fruit spectrum*. The descriptors used in the spectrum are guides only; you may have other terms in which you express particular varietal characters.

Mmm... could be a chardonnay

Example of the primary fruit spectrum for some varieties

RIESLING				
floral	citrus	lime	passionfruit	tropical fruit

SAUVIGNON BLANC					
asparagus	capsicum	herbaceous	grassy	gooseberry	tropical fruit

CHARDONNAY						
cucumber	grapefruit tobacco	apple gooseberry	lime	rockmelon melon	fruit salad peach	tropical fruit fig

PINOT NOIR					
cherry	strawberry	violets	raspberry	plum	stewed plum

CABERNET SAUVIGNON							
herbaceous	capsicum	tomato bush	leafy	minty	dusty	olive	black currant

SHIRAZ							
spicy	pepper	raspberry	plum	blackberry	mulberry	olive	jammy

EARLIER RIPENING STAGE →→→ LATER RIPENING STAGE

For any one vineyard there is a general association between the progression of aroma and flavour development in the berry and sugar accumulation. Descriptive characters at the early ripening stage are usually associated with lower sugar levels and those at the later stage appear as sugar ripening continues.

*H*owever aroma and flavour ripening does not necessarily progress through the whole spectrum in every situation. Some grapes will ripen to a stage where the characters are described more by those terms earlier in the spectrum, while others will ripen to a stage described by characters more in the middle or later in the spectrum. Variety, climate and grapegrowing practices all influence the types of aroma and flavour compounds (and their intensity) in the grapes at harvest.

Grapes of the same variety but from different vineyards can ripen to the same sugar level, but with different expressions of aroma and flavour.

Whether

a **Sauvignon Blanc** wine will have grassy, capsicum, tropical fruit, or other characters;

a **Chardonnay** wine will have tobacco, melony, peachy, or other characters;

a **Pinot Noir** wine will have strawberry, raspberry, plum, or other characters;

a **Cabernet Sauvignon** wine will have minty, herbaceous, blackcurrant, or other characters;

a **Shiraz** wine will have peppery, spicy, plum, mulberry, or other characters

depends on whether these characters were present in the grapes at harvest.

SITE 1 RIPENING PATTERN ONE	Sugar Level ° Baume	SITE 2 RIPENING PATTERN TWO
	13°	
PEACH/TROPICAL FRUIT/FIG	12°	MELON/PEACH
MELON/PEACH/TROPICAL FRUIT	11°	MELON
MELON/PEACH	10°	TOBACCO/MELON
TOBACCO/MELON	9°	CUCUMBER/TOBACCO/GRAPEFRUIT
CUCUMBER/TOBACCO/GRAPEFRUIT	8°	CUCUMBER
CUCUMBER	7°	UNRIPE CHARACTERS
UNRIPE CHARACTERS		UNRIPE CHARACTERS

Possible changes in aroma and flavour sensations of Chardonnay grapes during ripening under two ripening patterns.

Defining ripeness now takes on new dimensions. Viticulturists and winemakers refer to grapes not only as being *sugar ripe* (at the right sugar level), but also as being *flavour ripe* (having the right aroma and flavour compounds present in the grapes for the style of wine that they intend to make from those grapes). Flavour ripeness may occur at different sugar levels for different vineyards.

The varietal characters present in the grapes at harvest are carried over into the wine during winemaking and form a critical part of the style of the wine produced. The aromas and flavours of wines, particularly young wines, resemble those of the grape variety from which they were made.

Wine style commences in the vineyard, as this is where many characters of the wine originate.

As well as measuring the concentration of sugar and acid in the juice of the berries sampled from the vineyard, winemakers also appraise the types and intensity of varietal characters in those berries (normally by smelling and tasting the juice samples). They may be looking for the presence or absence of specific characters. This assessment, and the measurements of sugar and acid, are all taken into account in deciding when to harvest the vineyard.

Matching sugar and flavour ripeness requires not only an understanding of the principles of grape ripening, but also many years experience of assessing fruit and making wine from that vineyard. Traditional practices in certain vinegrowing regions reflect this knowledge that comes with time.

Winemakers are always mindful of the type and style of wine they plan to produce. Often wines from different vineyards and/or varieties will be blended to give a range of desirable characters, enhancing the interest and enjoyment of that wine.

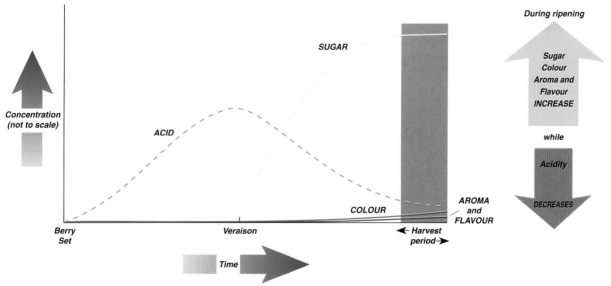

General changes in the composition of grapes as they ripen

*V*intage (the period of grape harvest and the beginning of winemaking) normally occurs in Australian vineyards during the months of February, March and April. It occurs at different times in different regions and for different varieties. Generally the warmer the region the earlier the commencement of vintage. For any one region the varieties Pinot Noir and Chardonnay are, as a rule, the first to reach a stage of ripeness suitable for harvest, while Cabernet Sauvignon is one of the last varieties to be harvested. The Hunter Valley region in New South Wales is often the first to finish vintage activities, while the cooler areas of Victoria and Tasmania can still be harvesting grapes into late April and early May.

At the stage of harvest the berries contain varying amounts of sugar, acid, colour and aroma and flavour compounds, as well as minerals and other nutrients - all the ingredients for making wine.

The exact time of harvest will depend on many factors, including not only the amounts and balance of these compounds but also the physical condition of the grapes and the prevailing weather conditions.

A general guide to the composition of grapes used to make the various types of wine.

Composition of the juice
(shown as typical ranges of values)

	Sugar (°Baumé)		Acidity (grams per litre)	
Table wines				
Sparkling wine	9 - 11		8 - 12	
Light-bodied dry white	10 - 12	LOW	7 - 9	HIGH
Full-bodied dry white	12 - 14		6 - 8	
Light-bodied dry red	10 - 12		7 - 9	
Full-bodied dry red	12 - 14		5 - 9	
Semi-sweet white wine	13 - 16		7 - 9	
Sweet white wine (eg, botrytis styles)	17 - 22		6 - 9	
Fortified wines				
Sherry	10 - 11	HIGH	6 - 9	
Port	14 - 16		4 - 6	
Muscat and Tokay	15 - 20		3 - 5	LOW

There will be a large range of grape colour and flavours that accompany the above values, which create different styles of wines within each wine type.

Seppelt... from grapes to wine.

THE WINERY

The making of the wine

$\mathcal{W}$inemaking is a dynamic process; many decisions need to be made during the life of every wine. In the following pages we discuss the steps in making white and red table wines, and particularly how the taste of the wine is influenced by the different processing techniques. We focus on the options available to winemakers in crafting the taste of their wines.

The production of sparkling and fortified wines involves variations of the processes discussed below and is covered in more detail later in the book.

Harvesting the grapes

Vintage is the period when the grapes are harvested and the wine is made.

The decision to remove the grapes from the vine is based on several factors, including:

- an assessment of the sugar/acid balance and the flavour profile of the grapes in relation to the style of wine to be produced;
- the prevailing weather conditions;
- the availability of labour and machinery;
- the condition of the grapes (whether the berries are shrivelling, or any disease is present).

Harvest commences when the winemaker considers that the grapes have ripened to the right stage for a particular style of wine.

Traditionally grapes have been hand-picked into baskets, buckets or crates, stacked and then transported from the vineyard to the winery by various means. Hand-picking removes whole bunches, leaving the berries attached to their stalks. While this practice still continues today, many of the larger vineyards are now picked by machines. We say that the grapes have been mechanically or machine harvested.

Mechanical harvesters operate by moving along the row and shaking the vines. The movement of the shoots causes the berries to be shaken off their stalks. The berries fall onto a conveyor belt contained in the machine and are carried by the moving belt to a bin for transport to the winery.

Compared to hand-pickers, these machines are able to pick grapes at a fraction of the cost and at greater speed, an advantage because the berries can be removed quickly when the fruit has reached the desired ripeness. Another advantage is that these machines can pick through the night; under these cooler conditions there is less oxidation (a term we discuss later) of the juice in the bottom of the container. The fruit arrives at the winery both cool and in good condition.

Mechanical harvesters cannot be used in situations where the vineyard is sited on steep slopes, or where the winemaking technique requires whole bunches of grapes, for example:

- in the production of premium sparkling wine, where whole bunch pressing is used to extract the juice;
- when red wines are made by the carbonic maceration method;

or

- where there is a need to select only parts of the bunches because disease is present.

Chardonnay grapes ready for processing at Heemskerk Winery in Tasmania.

Hand harvesting - the vertically shoot positioned canopy makes it easier to pick the bunches of grapes.

Shiraz grapes - ready for transport to the winery.

A Gregoire harvester working in the Yarra Valley at 4 o'clock in the morning.

The rods inside the machine that shake the vine and cause the berries to be shaken off their stalks.

Crushing

The grape berry must be broken to release its juice. The bunches (if hand-picked) or berries (if mechanically harvested) are normally crushed by passing them through a series of rollers which squash the berries and squeeze out the juice. The stalks (if present) are usually removed, and thus crushing produces a mixture of juice, pulp, skins and seeds, which we call *must*.

When harvested, the grapes will contain various proportions of sugar, acid, colour and aroma and flavour compounds. The winemaker can adjust the amount of sugar and acid to make the juice or must more suitable for a particular wine style.

Addition of sugar
The addition of sugar to juice or must is not permitted in Australia - an historic decision that was made when our vineyards were sited in mainly warm and hot climates. More recently many vineyards have been established in cooler regions and it seems logical that this law should be reconsidered in light of these developments. Grapes grown in cool climatic conditions may often attain preferred flavours at sugar levels slightly lower than desired, and it is here that some addition of sugar prior to fermentation may improve the sensory qualities of the resultant wine. The addition of sugar raises the alcohol level of the wine, improving its mouthfeel.

In cool to warm, warm, warm to hot and hot climatic regions, there is usually no need to modify the sugar content of the grapes, particularly if sound management practices have been used in their production.

In Australia the addition of grape juice concentrate is permitted and this can be used to raise the sugar content of the juice or must prior to fermentation; however this is considered to be a less satisfactory method than the addition of sugar.

Addition of acid
When grapes ripen in warm and hot climatic conditions there is more likely to be a deficiency of acid in the grapes at harvest, and it is more common that winemakers will need to adjust the acidity level of the juice or must prior to fermentation and/or during the winemaking process.

To do this, tartaric acid (one of the natural acids of the grape) is usually added.

Titratable acidity and pH
The concept of acidity was raised previously, in the section on grape ripening. Titratable acidity and pH are terms used to describe the acid conditions of grape juice or wine. Tartaric acid and malic acid are present in the grapes at harvest and are carried over into the wine. As well as these acids being present in wine, other acids may be formed by yeast and bacteria during winemaking, including lactic acid, acetic acid and succinic acid. In solutions such as grape juice or wine these acids can exist in different forms, one form being free hydrogen ions. Titratable acidity is a measure of all forms of all of the acids and gives an estimate of their overall concentration: how much acid (expressed as tartaric acid) is present in one litre of grape juice or wine. Values for titratable acidity in wine may be in the order of 6 to 10 grams of acid per litre. The concentration of acid relates to the acid taste of the wine, and generally the higher the titratable acidity, the more acidic the wine will taste.

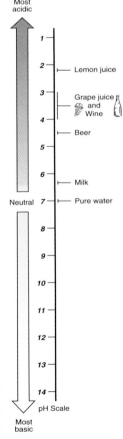

The pH scale and the pH values of some common beverages.

It is more difficult to grasp the concept of pH. It gives a measure of the concentration of only the free hydrogen ions, but these are important in that they influence chemical reactions in the juice or wine. However, the concentration of these in grape juice or wine is very low, in the order of 0.001 to 0.0001 grams of free hydrogen ions per litre. In order to express these very low values more conveniently, chemists invented the pH scale, not just for wine, but also for expressing the acid conditions of other solutions, such as other beverages and the water in your swimming pool. This scale covers the range from 0 to 14; values from 0 to 7 represent acidic solutions, and from 7 to 14 basic solutions. The lower the number on the pH scale, the higher the concentration of free hydrogen ions (ie, the more acidic the solution).

The lower the pH value of a juice or a wine, the less chance there is of oxidation and spoilage reactions occurring. Also, if the pH of a red wine is adjusted to a lower value (by the addition of acid) the wine will appear more red-coloured.

The pH value of grape juice and wine is normally in the range of pH 3 to pH 4, and even though this variation looks small, the differences in the chemical reactions and wine colour that occur in this range can be quite dramatic. Juices or wines at the higher pH values can oxidize very quickly. For this reason winemakers will adjust the pH to a lower value by the addition of tartaric acid, which also increases the titratable acidity. However, they must do this carefully and taste the wine after each addition, because if they add too much acid the wine will taste too acidic and thus out of balance. During the winemaking process, because of changes in the acid makeup of the wine, the pH will increase and thus winemakers need to check the pH value of the wine regularly and adjust if necessary. The aim is to achieve an acid level that is in balance with the sugar, alcohol and fruit sensations in any particular wine.

In summary
Titratable acidity measures the concentration of acid in the juice or wine and gives the winemaker some guide as to how acidic the wine will taste, while pH measures the chemical effectiveness of the acids present and gives the winemaker a guide as to how protected the wine is from oxidation and spoilage. Some chemists offer an analogy to a bank account, where titratable acidity gives a measure of the total amount of money in the account (capital + interest) whereas pH gives a measure of only the interest, and thus how effectively your account is operating.

Getting it right in the vineyard

Although winemakers can adjust the sugar/acid balance in the juice, must or wine, they cannot modify the main ingredients of style: the aromas and flavours of the grapes. This emphasises the importance of *getting it right in the vineyard*, ie, having the right amount and types of sugar, acid, colour, aroma and flavour present in the grapes at harvest. The best wines are often those made from grapes that require little or no adjustment of the juice or must components prior to fermentation.

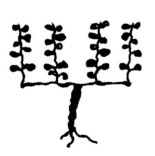

Oxidation
Oxidation is another word that is frequently used when discussing the winemaking process and wines. The term oxidation embraces the chemical, physical and sensory changes that occur in the juice or wine when it is exposed to air (oxygen), changes that include: a reduction of varietal aroma and flavour; the appearance of vinegar, nail polish remover and sherry-like smells; a browning of the colour; and the development of bitterness.

The wine is permanently damaged once these changes occur, since they are irreversible. This is why winemakers are so careful to avoid oxidation (in delicate dry white table wines) or to control it to a level where its influence is deemed as contributing to complexity (in some full-bodied white and red table wines). Controlled oxidation is in fact an integral part of the winemaking process for sherry style wines, which we discuss later, in the section covering fortified wines.

Oxidation occurs to a greater degree when air is readily absorbed, when the juice or wine is hot, when it has a high pH, and when the grapes are mouldy. Winemakers will minimize these conditions by using inert gas (nitrogen and/or carbon dioxide) in any pumping operations and to fill the head space in storage tanks, by keeping the juice or wine cool and by the addition of chemicals (sulphur dioxide and ascorbic acid) which inhibit the activity of micro-organisms and oxidizing enzymes and/or react with any air present.

Sulphur dioxide
Sulphur dioxide has been used in winemaking for many years; probably the Egyptians and Romans would have used it when making their wines. It is a unique compound in that it not only inhibits microbial activity, but also aids in preventing oxidation in wine. It is thus a very common and useful additive for maintaining the juice, must or wine in prime condition.

Sulphur dioxide can be added:
- to the bins in which the grapes are harvested and transported to the winery, preventing spoilage and oxidation of any juice in the bottom of the bin during transportation;
- to the juice or must prior to fermentation; and
- to the wine after fermentation and during storage.

Sulphur dioxide is only added in small amounts, and at these levels it is generally harmless to most wine consumers. A small proportion of consumers are sensitive to sulphur dioxide and may have adverse reactions when drinking wine. When sulphur dioxide has been added during winemaking, this will be indicated on the label by the code 220. The amount of sulphur dioxide added during white winemaking is normally higher than that required in processing red wines. Sweet white wines and cask wines will normally have higher levels of sulphur dioxide than bottled dry white wines, which will normally have higher levels than bottled dry red wines.

However, it is important to realize that sulphur dioxide is produced naturally by yeast during fermentation, and thus some sulphur dioxide will be present in wine even if it has not been added. People who are particularly sensitive are thus best advised to avoid drinking wine, unless they know that a particular wine has an extremely low level of sulphur dioxide and that they are not adversely affected by such wines.

Ascorbic acid
Ascorbic acid (a natural component of wine) may sometimes be added in white winemaking as it can react with any oxygen present in the juice or wine and thus prevent oxidation occurring. Again, the amounts added are very small. If ascorbic acid has been added to the wine during processing, the code 300 will appear on the label.

Pressing

In making white wines, the must is normally cooled immediately after crushing. It is then pumped to a draining vessel or to a press.

The juice that drains freely from either the draining vessel or the press is called the *free-run* juice. The remaining solids (pulp, skins and seeds) are pressed by some mechanical device to obtain more juice. Some of the juice obtained from the early stages of the pressing operation will be added to the free-run, while the juice obtained later in the cycle (when the pressing pressure is higher) may be discarded, because this fraction of the pressings may contain higher levels of compounds that impart bitter tastes in the final wine. After the pressing operation is

completed the dry mass of skins and seeds is discarded.

Grapes intended for the production of delicate white wine styles and premium sparkling wine may not necessarily be crushed prior to pressing. Pressing directly, as whole bunches, minimises pick up of phenolic compounds from the skin and seeds, which may otherwise have produced slightly bitter tastes in the final wine.

Making red wines requires a different approach to that used for white winemaking. The skins need to be kept in contact with the fermenting liquid, since they provide the red colour. The alcohol produced during the fermentation aids in the extraction of colour and tannins from the skins. The mixture of juice, pulp, skins and seeds is kept together and is not pressed until some stage during or after the fermentation.

In the making of red wine the skins need to be kept in contact with the fermenting liquid before pressing.

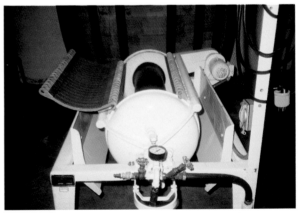

An air-bag press.
After the press is filled and the lid closed, the bag in the centre is filled with air, and, as it expands, it presses the material and releases the juice (or wine) from the mass of solid material. The juice or wine drains through slats in the press and is pumped to a storage or fermentation vessel.

Clarification of juice

Pressing only removes the larger particles from the juice or wine. Clarification is the removal of small solid particles (eg, skin debris) that have not been removed by the pressing operation.

Yeast settling to the bottom at the end of fermentation.

In white winemaking the white juice is allowed to stand while the small solid particles settle to the bottom of the tank. The clear juice (from above the solids) is then drawn off (*racked*) to the fermentation vessel. Additional clarification may be obtained by using centrifuges or filtration units. Sometimes winemakers will leave a small amount of solids in the juice during fermentation, and this may enhance the complexity of the resultant wine. This must be done with great care and after considerable experience, as too high an amount of solids will result in undesirable smells and coarse taste sensations in the finished wine. White wines are clarified again at the end of fermentation. In red winemaking the must is kept intact during fermentation and clarification occurs only at the end of this process.

Fermentation

Primary fermentation is the conversion by yeast of the sugar in the juice to alcohol and carbon dioxide.

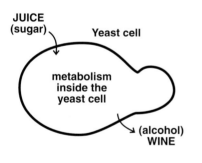

JUICE (sugar) — **Yeast cell** — **metabolism inside the yeast cell** — **(alcohol) WINE**

At the peak of fermentation there will be about 100 million of these cells in one ml of the fermenting liquid. It takes many yeast cells to make wine.

Like humans, yeast requires a balanced diet, so some other nutrients are often added to the ferment along with the yeast to ensure an efficient fermentation.

Specially selected yeast is normally added by the winemaker to the juice or must. Yeasts are selected on their ability to conduct the fermentation efficiently and on the sensory features they add to the wine. For example, some yeasts produce compounds that add to the fruity and estery characters of the wine, while others are more neutral, allowing greater expression of the varietal characters. This is a critical part of the winemaking process, and the widespread use of specially selected pure yeast strains in Australian winemaking has contributed significantly to the quality of our wines.

Fermentation of white wines

White wines are usually fermented in temperature controlled stainless steel vessels or in wooden (oak) barrels stored in a cold room to regulate temperature. Fermentation temperatures are generally in the range of 8-18°C. These conditions help to retain the varietal aromas and flavours of the grapes in the finished wine.

In the production of dry white table wines the fermentation is allowed to continue until all the sugar is fermented to alcohol, whereas for sweet white table wines the fermentation may be stopped part way through. This leaves some unfermented sugar present, which gives the wine its sweet taste. The fermentation is normally stopped by cooling the wine. Sweet white wines may also be produced by allowing the wine to ferment to dryness and then adding grape juice concentrate to sweeten the wine.

On the completion of fermentation, wines are stored in either stainless steel tanks or oak barrels.

Some grape varieties, particularly those such as Riesling and Traminer, which produce floral, fragrant wines, will be fermented and stored totally in stainless steel tanks.

Barrel fermentation and oak storage of white wines
Other varieties, such as Chardonnay, Semillon and Sauvignon Blanc, may be totally fermented in stainless steel tanks and then transferred to oak barrels, or they may be transferred to oak barrels part way through their fermentation, a process winemakers call *barrel fermentation*. Oak components are extracted into the wine, adding new aroma and flavour compounds.

Time on lees

With barrel fermentation, the wine can be retained in the barrel on the completion of fermentation and kept in contact with the dead yeast cells, creating further dimensions of aromas, flavours and mouth-feel sensations. Winemakers refer to this practice as *time on lees*. The length of time the wine remains on lees is at the discretion of the winemaker, but generally this may be from 2-12 months. Often Chardonnay wines will be treated in this way, with various combinations of barrel fermentation, time on lees and storage time in oak barrels being used to provide a range of blending options.

Wines that have also had time on lees will generally have improved mouth-feel, often described by saying that the wines have a creamy or cheesy texture on the palate. They also take on smells and tastes described as *creamy, yeasty, vegemite, bonox, marmite, cheesy, bready, toasty* and *leesy*.

The use of oak barrels in winemaking

During contact with oak barrels, whether it be during barrel fermentation or during storage, the wine takes on characters that are extracted from the oak wood. Some words frequently used to describe these oak characters include: *vanilla, toasty, sawdust, cedar, olives, spicy, bacon, coconut, pencil shavings, dusty, cashews, smoky, burnt, caramel, raisin* and *charred.*

While the wine is in barrels slow oxidation also occurs, modifying the wine even further.

A combination of all or some of the above practices creates what we call complexity in wine, ie, lots of different smells and tastes in harmony with each other.

People talk about wines being 'woody', 'oaky', 'showing lots of wood' or 'lots of oak' or 'good wood' or 'oak complexity', terms that are all associated with storing wine in oak barrels. Wood is the general term that encompasses the use of oak; the terms are often used interchangeably. Oak barrels have been used as storage vessels for wine for over 2000 years and winemakers have a choice of barrels made from eg, French, German or American oak. The oaks are named after the forests where they grow. You will hear winemakers talk about, for example, Nevers, Limousin and Troncais, which are different types of French oak.

The use of oak barrels is an expensive winemaking procedure (some barrels cost about $800 each) and thus wines treated in this way are more costly. To overcome this cost, oak chips or pieces of oak wood can be added to the wine during either fermentation or storage. This imparts the oak aroma and flavour to the wine, but does not produce the same complexity as fermenting or storing in oak barrels.

Malo-lactic fermentation (MLF)

A second fermentation can also occur in wines, which does not involve sugar or yeast. In this so-called secondary fermentation, bacteria convert the malic acid in the wine to lactic acid. The bacteria are those naturally present in the wine environment or specially selected strains added by the winemaker. Grapes grown in cold and/or cool environments may contain high levels of malic acid which, when carried over into the wine, will make the wine taste too acidic. Winemakers can choose to put these wines through a malo-lactic fermentation. The lactic acid formed has a less acid taste than the malic acid, and the conversion thus results in a better acid balance in the wine; the wine tastes softer on the palate.

In addition, other chemical compounds are formed during the conversion which give the wine smell and taste sensations described by words such as *creamy, buttery, butterscotch, yogurt* and *caramel.*

Winemakers now use the technique of MLF for many of their wines, not just those produced from grapes that come from cool climates. It is used often for Chardonnay wines to give flavour enhancement and to improve complexity and mouthfeel.

A view of an oak forest in the Troncais region of France.

Logs ready for transport.

Splitting the logs.

Open air storage of staves.

Assembling and firing the cask.

Bending the cask.

The finished product.

The making of oak barrels

Oak forests are grown in parts of France, Germany, other European countries and the United States of America. Once the tree is cut, the log is taken to the mill where it is split by the millers into staves. The staves are then either kiln or air dried, a process called seasoning. If the staves are not seasoned to the appropriate moisture level they may dry out after they have been made into barrels; then the joints between the staves will separate and the barrel will leak. The seasoning process may take up to 3 years.

When the oak is deemed ready for processing into barrels, the staves are cut to length and then a sufficient number is selected for the type of barrel. The set of staves is then placed inside a hoop which holds the unbent staves at one end. This is called 'raising the barrel'. After raising, the barrel is ready to be bent. This is achieved by placing the set of unbent staves over a fire, which is normally fuelled by oak pieces. By constantly wetting the staves with water, steam is produced, which renders the staves pliable. Over a period of about 30 minutes, the barrel can then be shaped by placing a wire around the bottom end, which is winched into shape while being heated. When the bending is complete, the barrel is returned to the open fire for another 30 minutes to 1 hour. The inside of the barrel becomes toasted to various degrees, depending on how long it is left over the fire.

After the barrel is removed from the fire and cooled, the heads (ends) are fitted, and new hoops are then rivetted, fitted and driven into the barrel. It is now ready to be filled with wine.

Oak barrels come in a variety of sizes:

Quarter casks - 160 litres
Barriques - 225 litres
Hogsheads - 300 litres
Puncheons - 475 litres

and in some cases, much larger vats.

These pictures show the barrel making process at C.A. Schahinger Pty Ltd, Master Coopers in Adelaide, South Australia.

Oak Barrels

Fermentation of red wines

Fermentation temperature

Fermentation at a cool temperature (below 20°C) retains fruit characters and limits the extraction not only of colour and tannins from the skins, but also of bitter tannins from the seeds.

Higher fermentation temperatures (above 20°C) are required to extract more flavour, colour and tannins from the skins. More tannins may also be extracted from the seeds. Sometimes earthy and more complex characters are associated with hotter fermentations.

The fermentation process generates heat and therefore the fermenting liquid must be cooled to maintain the desired fermentation temperature range. Cooling and maceration operations are often combined.

Maceration techniques

As the fermentation progresses, carbon dioxide and alcohol are formed. The carbon dioxide gas pushes the mixture of skins and seeds to the top of the fermenting liquid. The alcohol produced in the fermenting liquid helps to extract the colour from the skins; therefore the cap of skins must be kept in contact with the liquid by frequent mixing. There are various methods for mixing the cap with the fermenting liquid and we discuss some of the alternatives below.

Pumping over: pumping liquid from the bottom of the tank and splashing or jetting it over the top of the cap. As the liquid leaches through the cap it extracts the colour from the skins. The liquid can also be cooled as it is pumped, thus controlling the temperature of the fermentation.

Pumping over a red wine fermentation at St Hallett Winery in the Barossa Valley.

Plunging down: pushing the cap down into the liquid with a plunger. This may be carried out a couple of times a day. An interesting variation is for people to stand on top of the cap and gently work a hole in it by moving their feet up and down, gradually pushing all the cap down into the liquid.

Treading a Pinot Noir fermentation at Henschke's Winery.

Heading down: placing boards across the tank (towards the top of the tank). The cap is trapped below the boards but the liquid can rise between the gaps (or through a central riser tube). The skins are then always in contact with the liquid. The liquid is also pumped over regularly during the fermentation.

Rotary Fermenters: vessels that look something like rotating cement mixers. After crushing, the mixture of juice, skins and seeds is pumped into the tank, the lid closed and the tank rotated regularly to keep the skins submerged in the liquid. This procedure enhances the extraction of flavour, colour and tannins in a short time.

A Vinimatic rotary fermenter.

Time on skins

A short time on skins produces lighter coloured, more fruity styles, eg, rosé or light-bodied reds. Longer skin contact increases flavour, colour and tannin extraction. At fermentation temperatures around 25°C, most of the flavour and colour is extracted from the skins by about midway through the fermentation, while tannin extraction continues for as long as the skins and seeds are kept in contact with the liquid. When the winemaker considers that the right balance between flavour, colour and tannins has been reached, the partly fermented wine will be drained off to another tank to finish fermentation. The wine obtained from this draining process is called the free run. The mass of skins and seeds is then pressed to recover more wine (called the *pressings*), which may or may not be added to the free run; it all depends on the quality of the pressings. A normal period of skin contact would be about 4-6 days.

Extended Skin Contact

Some wines will be left in contact with the skins and seeds for much longer than this, even after the fermentation is complete, sometimes for up to 4 weeks, before they are drained and pressed. Winemakers refer to this as *extended skin contact*. This can produce a more complex wine, stabilise the colour and often soften the astringency of the tannins.

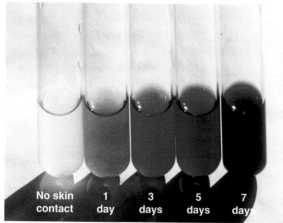

An example of the colour of wines made from the same fermentation but with different times of skin contact.

Barrel fermentation

Some free run wine may be transferred part way through fermentation to oak barrels to complete fermentation.Winemakers consider that this induces a more subtle integration of the oak and barrel fermentation characters into the wine.

A traditional basket press in Rockford's winery in the Barossa Valley.

Pressing

The pressings will normally be more highly coloured and tannic and, as the pressing continues, more bitter. The quality of the wine from the pressing stage is influenced largely by the maceration technique. Pressings from wines that have been fermented hot and/or heavily macerated are less suitable for adding to the free run. Often the wine from the last stages of the pressing operation, where higher pressures are used to extract the liquid, may be more bitter and will be kept separate.

Gentle maceration combined with gentle pressing is an ideal approach to produce flavoursome, medium-bodied wines which still have good tannin sensation and a soft, pleasing mouthfeel.

Storage in oak barrels

Most red wines will be stored for some time in oak barrels. They take on new sensory characters that come from the oak barrels. During oak storage there is slow uptake of oxygen and developed (aged) characters may appear in the wine, which integrate with the oak and primary fruit characters. The wine is stored in the barrel until the winemaker considers that the balance is right; storage time may vary from a few months to two years or more.

Malo-lactic fermentation (MLF)

Most red wines (except for rosé and light-bodied styles) will be put through a malo-lactic fermentation. The influence of these characters may not be as obvious as it is in white wines. There are changes in the sensory characters but they are difficult to describe. However, because of the decrease in acidity occurring during the malo-lactic conversion, the wines will feel softer on the palate and will be more pleasant to drink.

Maturation

Wines that are meant to be consumed while they are young (eg, most aromatic white wines and light-bodied red wines) will be bottled soon after they are made. Others, predominantly full-bodied white and red wines, may be matured in new or used oak barrels before they are bottled. Primary fruit flavours are gradually transformed to *developed (aged) characters*; white wines may take on *toasty, honey, nutty, cashew* and *kerosene types of characters*, and red wines may develop *gamey, meaty, earthy, leathery, mushroom, dusty, cowyard, barnyard, cigar box, licorice, chocolate* or *coffee-like* characters.

Wood characters (if present) harmonize with primary and developed fruit sensations. Red wines become browner and whites more golden. Astringency (in reds) decreases as tannins become larger and the wine appears softer on the palate and more pleasurable to drink. Apparent sweetness (from fruit and alcohol) may become more obvious.

All these balances change with time, both while the wine is stored in the tanks or barrels in the cellar and then while the wine is in the bottle.

White wines develop more yellow/golden colours with time.

Red wines become more red/brown and brown with time.

Clarification, fining and stabilisation of wine

After primary fermentation the wine is left to settle and then the clear wine is racked from the yeast lees at the bottom of the tank. Further clarification of the wine can occur through centrifuging or filtering.

Stabilisation is the removal of unstable compounds which may otherwise form a haze or deposit in the bottled wine. This ensures that the wine will be bright and free of deposits when enjoyed by the consumer.

Unstable proteins which can form a haze in the wine are removed by the addition of a natural clay compound called bentonite, which combines with the protein and settles to the bottom of the tank to give clear wine. In some bottles of wine you may see a small deposit of crystals, particularly after the bottle has been stored in the refrigerator.

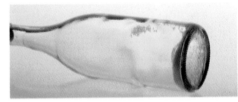

Unstable tartrate crystals settling on the inside of the bottle.

These are tartrate crystals, a natural part of the wine; they precipitate out under cool conditions. They are not harmful and a small amount of these crystals is acceptable. However, most consumers prefer their white wine to be perfectly clear. To ensure this winemakers will, after fermentation and usually after any blending operations, chill the wine and hold it at about minus 3°C to precipitate out all or most of the unstable tartrate crystals before the wine is bottled. This process is called *cold-stabilisation*.

Many red wines are not filtered and cold stabilised to the same extent as white wines. Thus, in some red wines, crystals of tartrate and sediments of coloured tannins may appear in the wine as it ages. These are natural products and are not harmful. They can easily be removed by decanting the wine prior to serving.

During the period from the end of fermentation to bottling, the winemaker may refine the taste of the wine by the addition of fining agents, such as gelatine, casein and egg white, which react with and remove phenolic compounds in the wine which would otherwise give bitter and coarse tastes. In using these agents the winemaker is further fine-tuning the structure of the wine.

Blending

Some wines are made from one grape variety harvested from one vineyard, but many wines are the result of blending different wines: wines from different varieties, wines from different vineyards and even wines of different ages.

Winemakers mix the different wines in order to achieve a certain wine style, relying on their tasting abilities to indicate the mix which will give the most enjoyable taste.

Components of each wine in the blend contribute complexity, balance and structure, creating an improved wine overall.

We cover aspects of blending in more detail when discussing wine styles later in the book.

The decision to bottle

The winemaker is continually making decisions throughout the winemaking process to ensure that the wine fits the desired style and that it is ready for bottling: *how to ferment? whether and how long to store in oak barrels? will a malo-lactic be beneficial? cold stabilisation? fining? filtering? when to bottle?*

The winemaker constantly tastes the wine and decides how a particular wine will be treated depending on an assessment of how the above operations will influence the taste of the wine. It is a continual process of crafting and fine-tuning the taste of each wine, each step in the winemaking process linking the wine more closely with its maker.

Bottling

When the winemaker decides that the wine is ready for bottling, it will be checked for clarity and stability and then filtered into a bottle or cask. Most white wines, particularly sweet white wines, will be sterile filtered into their container, which ensures that the wine will be free of any yeast or bacteria that could grow in the wine after bottling. Red wines are usually filtered, but not to the same degree of sterility as white wines. Reds contain low amounts of sugar, have normally undergone a malo-lactic fermentation, and have been stored for longer periods of time. Thus the chance of any yeast or bacterial activity occurring after bottling is low.

The aim of the bottling process is to maintain the quality of the wine. Very sophisticated bottling lines are used in the wine industry to sterile filter the wine and also to protect it from oxidation during bottling.

The bottle is then sealed with either a cork or a screw cap. Cork is the more common method.

A wine cork comes from the bark of cork-oak trees. The laborious task of harvesting the bark in a forest in Portugal is illustrated above. It takes about 12 years for the bark to regrow.

The finished product: a cylinder of cork cut from the bark.

Once the wine is bottled and sealed, the next step is to label and package the product. This is all part of the image of the wine that the winemaker wishes to portray to the consumer.

Wine from Penley Estate, one of the newer wineries based in Coonawarra, Australia's most famous red wine district.

Maturation in the bottle

Some wines, mainly full-bodied whites and reds, will benefit from being allowed to mature in the bottle prior to drinking, more time being required for the integration of primary fruit, developed fruit and oak characters, and in red wines for the tannins to soften.

Each wine will be perfected in its own time.

Wine should be stored on its side, in a place with constant temperature (preferably about 13ºC) and humidity (about 90%), and which is dark and free from odours.

Care for your wine.

Some wines will be ready to be enjoyed when young, sometimes within a year of their making, while others will require many years to reach perfection.

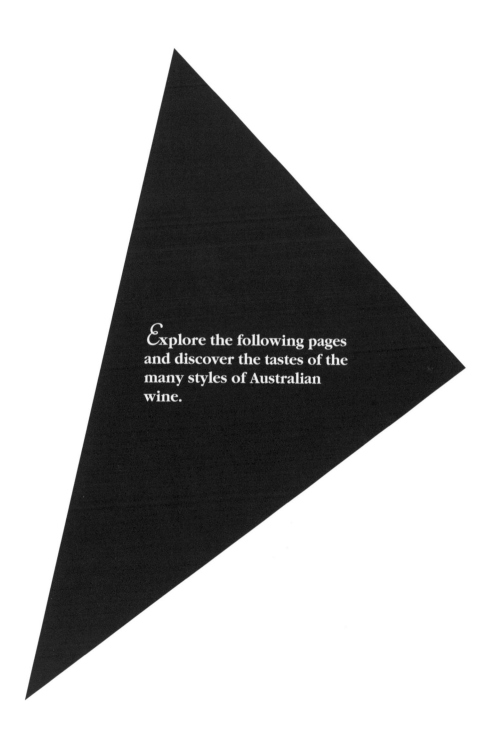

Explore the following pages and discover the tastes of the many styles of Australian wine.

The vines of Domaine Chandon in the Yarra Valley.

Sparkling wine

Sparkling wines, traditionally the wines of celebration, bring atmosphere to an occasion. These are wines where the senses of sight, smell and taste are used to their fullest, from the excitement of the bubbles through to the crisp acidity and subtle, lingering flavours on the palate.

Whether the wine is from a Champagne House or an Australian wine company, creating a distinctive style is what sparkling wine is all about. While the Champagne Houses have had hundreds of years to develop their style, Australian sparkling wine producers are only at the beginning of their search for distinctiveness, and names such as Croser, Yalumba D, Salinger, Domaine Chandon and Yellowglen are building a quality image and reputation for the Australian style of sparkling wine.

This style shows the development of flavours that come from our vineyards and winemaking philosophy. The establishment of new vineyards in cooler regions of Australia, the refinement of winemaking philosophy and experience with blending are all contributing to the goals of each company in achieving a distinctive *House Style* in their wines.

Sparkling wines may be produced by a variety of means, varying from the intricate *Méthode Champenoise* process down to the simple infusion of carbon dioxide bubbles into a still table wine, both of which we will explain in the following pages. We will also introduce you to a great range of sparkling wines, including the classic Australian wine style of *Sparkling Burgundy.*

The making of sparkling wine - the intricacies of Méthode Champenoise (the traditional French method)

Choice of grape varieties

Premium sparkling wine is made from various combinations of the grape varieties Chardonnay, Pinot Noir and Pinot Meunier.

Harvesting the grapes

Bunches of grapes are normally picked in the earlier stages of ripening, when sugar levels are about 10 to 11° Baumé, when acid levels are high (about 9 to 12 grams per litre as tartaric acid) and when the grapes show desirable aroma and flavour characteristics.

As the Australian sparkling wine industry has developed, it has become evident that the most desirable characters are found in grapes grown in cooler regions. Nevertheless, warmer areas are able to provide quality fruit for the commercial sparkling wine styles. By picking the fruit in the earlier stages of ripening, juice with good acid and some appealing characters can be obtained. Often fruit from warmer climates will not have the intensity of the right types of characters and/or the structure suitable for longer ageing on yeast lees. Wines made from these grapes are released early and are often described as having more primary fruit characters and being less complex, but they can still be refreshing, flavoursome and enjoyable.

Cooler climates bring out the best features of Chardonnay, Pinot Noir and Pinot Meunier for the making of premium quality sparkling wines. Grown under these conditions, the grapes have high natural acidity, a high intensity of desirable varietal characters, and good structure, features which after long ageing on yeast lees produce sparkling wines with rich but subtle and complex flavours and alluring creamy textures. It is difficult to describe the desirable varietal characters in the grapes at harvest. They are very delicate and are associated with the early to mid stages of the ripening spectrum for each variety. Winemakers often use descriptors such as grapefruit, green apples, lemon, tobacco and melon to describe Chardonnay, but it is really the overall structure (high acid and intensity of delicate flavours) that is important. It is often easier to recognise desirable characters at the end of primary fermentation than in the fruit. It is at this stage that the different wines are selected for their suitability to contribute to blends for making particular sparkling wine styles.

Once the decision to pick the grapes is made, they are hand picked into crates and then often stored in a coldroom prior to pressing.

Pressing

Whole bunches of grapes are pressed as gently as possible so that there is minimal contact between the grape skins and seeds and the expressed juice. This avoids extraction of phenolic compounds (which may cause bitterness) from these parts of the berries, and with black grape varieties avoids any leakage of colour from the skins into the juice. The pressing operation can be carried out with traditional presses or with modern presses which often utilize computer controlled programmes to regulate the pressures. This gentle pressing can produce clear juice even from the black grape varieties Pinot Noir and Pinot Meunier.

The juice that is released first contains the most sugar, acid and desirable flavour compounds and the least pickup of phenolic compounds. As the pressure is increased during the pressing cycle, the composition of the pressed juice changes. It becomes less acidic and more phenolic, and with black grapes more colour is extracted from the skins.

The juice obtained from the different stages of the pressing cycle is drawn off and stored in separate vessels; there may be three or more separate fractions. The juice from the first stages of pressing is more suitable for the production of high quality sparkling wine.

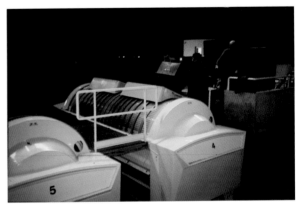

A modern press. Winemakers can choose to use either modern presses or traditional Champagne presses to extract the juice from the berries. Both systems can provide gentle and efficient pressing of the grapes.

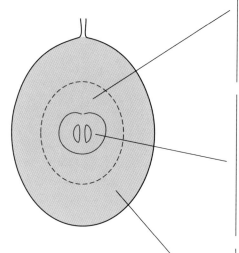

The first pressing releases the juice from the mid-section of the berry. It is:

- the most easily extracted
- the richest in sugar
- the richest in acid
  and
- the lowest in phenolics.

The second pressing (or as the pressure is increased) releases juice from the section closest to the seeds. It is:

- harder to extract
- lower in sugar
- lower in acid
  and
- higher in phenolics.

The third pressing (or as the pressure is increased further) releases the juice that is nearest to the skin. It is:

- even harder to extract
- even lower in sugar
- even lower in acid
- sometimes 'oily' in flavour
  and
- even higher in phenolics.

Pinot Noir grapes ready to be transferred to the press.

A traditional Champagne press at Padthaway Estate Winery in the south-east of South Australia. It is the only one of its type in Australia and is housed in an old shearing shed which has been converted to the Woolshed Winery. It adds to the atmosphere you experience when visiting Padthaway Estate, especially during the vintage period.

Primary fermentation (creating the base wines)

Each batch of juice is clarified, yeast is added and the juice then fermented in a similar way to a normal white wine fermentation. The resultant wines are called *base wines*. The winemaker thus ends up with at least three base wines from each pressing operation. The different pressings from the different grape varieties and from each vineyard are usually stored and fermented separately. Makers of sparkling wine thus have many different wines in their cellars at the end of vintage, giving them many options in the blending process that follows.

Imagine there are ten vineyards (five Chardonnay vineyards, four Pinot Noir vineyards and one Pinot Meunier vineyard) from which grapes are sourced for sparkling wine production. If each vineyard is harvested separately and the grapes pressed to obtain three juice fractions and if they are fermented separately into wine, thirty different base wines would be obtained in all.

Additionally, the base wines may be made in many different ways, influencing their structure and suitability for blending for certain sparkling wine styles. Yeast selection, fermentation temperature, the degree of clarification of the juice prior to fermentation and the type of fermentation vessel (stainless steel or oak vats) are some of the options that winemakers have in moulding the structure of their base wines. Some winemakers also put varying portions of their base wines through a malo-lactic fermentation, the flavours of which may carry through to the final wine.

Because base wines are quite acidic, the malo-lactic fermentation also softens the palate due to a decrease in perceived acidity.

Wineries producing sparkling wine may make up to a hundred (or even more) base wines, representing the many varieties, vineyards, pressing fractions and winemaking variations.

Blending - the art of making sparkling wine

After vintage, all the base wines are assembled and assessed. Various combinations of the different base wines are made up so that the winemaker can decide which is the best blend for the style of sparkling wine to be produced.

The blend of the different wines is called the *cuvée*. The cuvée may not be made up of only the current year's wine but may be modified by the use of *reserve wine* (wine kept from previous years). The task of blending requires a great deal of skill and experience as it is the characters of the cuvée that dictate the structure and style of the finished sparkling wine. The blender must almost be able to look into the future and anticipate how the blend will develop and how it will then fit the desired style of sparkling wine.

With many different base wines available the winemaker strives to combine their individual flavours and structural components so that a cuvée is assembled that will produce a sparkling wine of the desired House Style(s) and brand names.

If 85% or more of the cuvée comes from the current vintage, the final wine may be labelled as *Vintage*.

If a significant proportion of reserve wine is added in structuring the cuvée, the final wine must be labelled as *Non Vintage* or without any indication of the year.

The Cuvée

If the cuvée is made up of wine made from Pinot Noir, the final wine may be labelled *Blanc de Noir*.

If the cuvée is made up of wine made from Chardonnay grapes, the final wine may be labelled *Blanc de blanc*.

If some red wine (made from Pinot Noir) is added to the cuvée, or if some skin contact is allowed during the making of the base wine from Pinot Noir, the final wine may be labelled *Rosé*.

Secondary fermentation (creating the bubbles)

After the composition of the cuvée is decided, the selected wines are mixed with an amount of sugar (about 22 grams per litre), yeast and some other additives and then transferred to heavy-weight, pressure-tested bottles. These are the bottles in which the secondary fermentation will take place and in which the wine will be sold.

Each bottle is crown sealed and stored on its side. The small amount of sugar is converted by the yeast to alcohol and carbon dioxide gas, which is trapped in the bottle giving the wine its bubbles. The alcohol content of the wine is raised by about 1.5%v/v.

Sugar + Yeast ➔ Alcohol + Carbon Dioxide
(the bubbles)

The secondary fermentation occurs in the bottle.

The secondary fermentation lasts approximately six weeks; then the yeast cells die and settle on the inside of the bottle. The bottles are then stored for a further period of time, sometimes up to three years or even longer. This period is referred to as *storage on yeast lees*. It is during this storage period that the wine slowly ages and the primary fruit characters of the cuvée evolve into new sensations that we call developed fruit characters. The wine can take on bready, biscuity, meaty, toasty, honey and nut-like characters. After some months the yeast cells start to break down (*yeast autolysis*),

releasing flavour compounds into the wine which interact with those formed during the ageing process. Yeast autolysis often produces sensory characters that we associate with bread, biscuits, nuts and vegemite. Some of the words are similar to those we use for describing developed fruit characters.

The quality of sparkling wine is largely dependent on the development of fruit characters, which give subtle and complex flavours and structure to the palate. Yeast autolysis characters complement these changes in the fruit profile.

High quality sparkling wines benefit from a longer time on yeast lees, since the cuvée from which they were made would have contained many desirable flavours that develop with time and benefit from interaction with the flavours from yeast autolysis. These wines may spend from two to five years on yeast lees, allowing greater time for the merging of aged and yeast autolysis characters. Apart from these aroma and flavour changes, the wine can take on a creamy texture, giving a very pleasing sensation on the palate.

Sparkling wines made from cuvées of lower quality are usually stored for a shorter period (six months to two years), since they do not contain a high concentration of components which will improve with age. These wines do not necessarily improve by being left on yeast lees for longer periods. Some, in fact, will be removed from the yeast lees even before yeast autolysis occurs.

The drives at Seppelt Great Western Winery, where the wines slowly develop their sparkling wine character under constant cool temperature conditions.

Remuage
(moving the yeast lees to the neck of the bottle)

When the winemaker considers that the wine has developed the characters of the desired style, it is necessary to remove the yeast lees from the bottle to obtain a clear sparkling wine product. The bottles are shaken and transferred to either a special wooden frame or a mechanical remuage machine for the *remuage* (riddling) procedure. This aims to shake the yeast lees to the neck of the bottle in the minimum time and without leaving yeast lees sediment either in solution or as streak marks down the side of the bottle.

The remuage process is carried out on an A-shaped wooden frame, which normally has sixty slots on each side. The frame holds ten dozen bottles overall. The remueur follows a pattern in which each bottle is lifted, shaken, turned and replaced on the rack, normally twice a day. Each bottle is usually turned an eighth of a turn (45°) clockwise each time and is gradually raised so that its position on the rack becomes more vertical. The sediment is observed after each operation to check that it is being effectively shaken down towards the neck of the bottle. This procedure goes on for about twenty days until the sediment has moved into the neck of the bottle.

Each batch of sparkling wine may require a slightly different remuage pattern. The job of the remueurs is a very skilful one, and once experienced they can often manipulate thousands of bottles in a day. All this adds to the atmosphere and tradition of sparkling wine production. The work is very laborious, and it takes a long time to process a large number of bottles. Therefore it can be readily appreciated why some companies have moved (in part or totally) to the use of mechanical means of carrying out the remuage process, such as gyropallettes.

Recently winemakers have also been experimenting with the use of yeast encapsulated in alginate beads. These porous beads are placed inside each bottle; the sugar in the wine can diffuse into the beads, where it is converted to alcohol and carbon dioxide which then pass out of the beads back into the wine, but the yeast and subsequent yeast lees remain inside the bead. At the end of the secondary fermentation the bottle is inverted and the beads fall to the neck of the bottle where they can easily be removed. With time this may become a common method for conducting the secondary fermentation.

Yeast lees settled on the lower side of the bottle during storage.

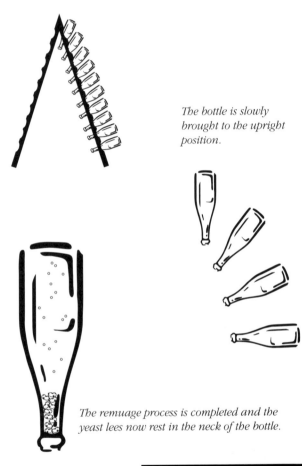

The bottle is slowly brought to the upright position.

The remuage process is completed and the yeast lees now rest in the neck of the bottle.

The remuage process can be carried out mechanically by the use of gyropallettes.

62

The cellars of Domaine Chandon.

*D*isgorging
(removing the yeast lees)

At this stage the bottle is fully inverted and the yeast lees have settled into the neck of the bottle, leaving clear wine above. The neck of the bottle is immersed in a freezing solution (approximately minus 30°C), which has the effect of freezing the plug of yeast lees into a solid mass. The bottle is then turned upright and the crown seal removed. The internal bottle pressure derived from the carbon dioxide produced in the secondary fermentation is sufficient to expel the frozen plug of yeast lees out of the neck of the bottle. Because the wine is cold there is minimum loss of pressure during this operation. It can be done either manually or, more commonly, by machines which form part of the bottling operation.

Some winemakers release a wine onto the market at various stages, eg, when it has had three, five or more years on yeast lees, and to indicate that the wine has only recently been disgorged it may be labelled 'RD' (recently disgorged). This indicates that it is different from the first or previous releases; for example the 1987 Croser was released as a vintage wine in 1989 and then as an 'RD' style in 1992 and 1993.

Dosage, bottling and packaging

After disgorgement, each bottle is topped up with the same wine and is usually sweetened by the addition of a sugar/wine solution (*liqueur*) to a pre-determined sweetness level appropriate for the style. A sparkling wine that is labelled *brut* (indicating a dry style) will have about 12 grams of sugar per litre, while other styles will have between about 15 and 30 grams of sugar per litre, depending on the particular wine. Each company has its own special recipe for this dosage addition; sometimes a touch of brandy or reserve wine will be added as well as sugar. These aid in maintaining the style of the particular sparkling wine.

The bottle is then corked, and a wire strap (*muselet*) is placed over the cork and tightened around the neck of the bottle. The wiring prevents the cork ejecting as the wine warms up or as the cork shrinks in the bottle over time.

The bottle is shaken to mix the dosage addition into the wine, and then the bottle is labelled and packaged.

Croser - one of Australia's premium sparkling wines.

Storage of the packaged wine

Sparkling wine is ready to drink when it is released on the market, as it is at this stage that the winemaker considers the wine to be at its best, reflecting the harmony of all the steps in its making. If stored for too long a period the wine will slowly develop additional characters, associated with bottle age, which may or may not complement the other characters of the wine. It is difficult to predict how each wine will be affected, but generally sparkling wine should be consumed soon after its release and at least within a year or two. Sparkling wines, with very few exceptions, are not wines to be stored for long periods of time in your cellar.

Trust the winemakers in their decision as to when the wine is ready to be enjoyed.

Sparkling wine corks - before insertion into the bottle (left) and how the cork can change shape over approximately two years in the bottle.

*O*ther ways to make sparkling wine

• *The transfer system*

This is a modification of the Méthode Champenoise process. The secondary fermentation still occurs in a bottle but at the end of the period on yeast lees, rather than each bottle being treated individually, the contents of the bottles are transferred under counter pressure to a pressure tank. The wine is mixed and filtered (to remove the yeast lees), dosage is added and then the wine is filled into new bottles. The main advantage of this process is that it avoids the time and labour of the remuage operation and provides for greater uniformity in the finished wine. The wine can be labelled 'bottle fermented' but it cannot be labelled 'fermented in this bottle' as in Méthode Champenoise wines.

Wines made in this manner cover a wide range of quality from large commercial brands to premium sparkling wine; the major difference is the grape varieties used to make each wine. The higher quality wines are made from the classic grape varieties (Chardonnay, Pinot Noir and Pinot Meunier), and these wines can show similar characters and qualities to those made by the Méthode Champenoise process.

• *Charmat process (fermentation in tanks)*

The base wines, sugar and yeast are mixed in large refrigerated pressure tanks. The secondary fermentation occurs in these tanks and then, after a period of time on yeast lees, the wine is sweetened, filtered (under pressure) and bottled. Grape varieties other than the classic varieties are usually included in the blend.

• *Carbonated*

The base wine blend is sweetened with sugar, filtered, chilled and infused with carbon dioxide gas in large refrigerated pressure tanks. It is then bottled under a counter-pressure filling system.

Grape varieties other than the classic varieties may be used in the blend. The wines are often sweet and fruity, with large bubbles which dissipate quickly.

Different ways to make sparkling wine

Méthode Champenoise	Transfer process	Charmat process	Carbonated
Usually classic varieties	Usually classic varieties	Mix of classic and other varieties	Mix of classic and other varieties
↓	↓	↓	↓
Usually hand picked grapes	Hand or machine picked grapes	Hand or machine picked grapes	Hand or machine picked grapes
↓	↓	↓	↓
Primary fermentation	Primary fermentation	Primary fermentation	Primary fermentation
↓	↓	↓	↓
Blending process	Blending process	Blending process	Blending process
↓	↓	↓	↓
Transfer to bottles	Transfer to bottles	Transfer to pressure tanks	Filtering and transfer to pressure tanks
↓	↓	↓	↓
Secondary fermentation in individual bottles	Secondary fermentation in individual bottles	Secondary fermentation occurs in pressure tanks	No secondary fermentation; carbon dioxide gas is bubbled into the wine in the pressure tank. The wine is sweetened and mixed
↓	↓	↓	
Remuage	Transfer (under pressure) of contents of each bottle to a pressure tank, where they are sweetened and mixed	Clarified and transferred under pressure to a pressure tank where it is sweetened and mixed	
↓	↓	↓	↓
Disgorgement and liqueuring			
↓	↓	↓	↓
	Filtration	Filtration	Filtration
	↓	↓	↓
Bottling (in the same bottle in which secondary fermentation occurred)	Bottling (in a different bottle to which secondary fermentation occurred)	Bottling	Bottling
↓	↓	↓	↓
Packaging	Packaging	Packaging	Packaging

Méthode Champenoise -

*A*ustralian premium sparkling wines are made from Chardonnay, Pinot Noir and Pinot Meunier grapes sourced from selected cool climate sites across the southern regions of Australia.

Grown in these cool climates and with sound vineyard management, the grapes have high natural acidity, intense desirable varietal characters and features that lead to improved structure in the finished wine; often winemakers will describe these types of wines as being 'tight' in flavour and structure.

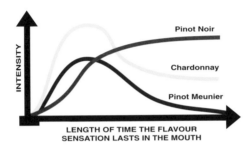

LENGTH OF TIME THE FLAVOUR
SENSATION LASTS IN THE MOUTH

In the finished wine, Chardonnay and Pinot Meunier flavour sensations are apparent earlier than those of Pinot Noir, whose stronger flavours develop in the mouth with time. Both Chardonnay and Pinot Noir contribute to length and persistence.

The cuvée must be made up with a view to how each component will change during the period the wine is stored on yeast lees.

<u>Each component of the blend contributes
special features</u>

Chardonnay - added to the blend to provide finesse and elegance. Great potential for long ageing on yeast lees.

Pinot Noir - the backbone of many sparkling wines, providing fullness, weight and length to the palate. Great potential for long ageing on yeast lees.

Pinot Meunier - added to some blends to provide fruitiness and roundness.

The harmony of it all

These are some of the characters you may find in sparkling wines

Primary fruit characters	Characters that develop during storage on yeast lees	Other characters
	(Some will be developed fruit characters, others will be derived from yeast autolysis. Often these words represent the synergy between these two influences)	(These might be present due to modifications to base wines eg, malo-lactic conversion, solids fermentation)
lemons, citrus, grapefruit, tobacco, apples, melons, figs, floral, fruity, perfumed, strawberry, confectionery	yeasty, doughy, freshly baked bread, crusty bread rolls, bready, toasty, biscuity, meatiness, cold roast lamb, bonox, vegemite, marmite, cashew, hazelnut, nutty, figgy, creamy, coconut, caramel, nougat, honey, honeycomb, almond, mushroom, truffle	creamy, buttery, leesy, cheesy, crushed biscuits, nutty

*During this period the wine develops features
that give pleasing, creamy mouthfeel*

The actual characters present in any one wine will depend on the style of that wine.
Wines may have a few or many of these characters.

d The Taste Of The Wine

THE WINEMAKING PROCESS

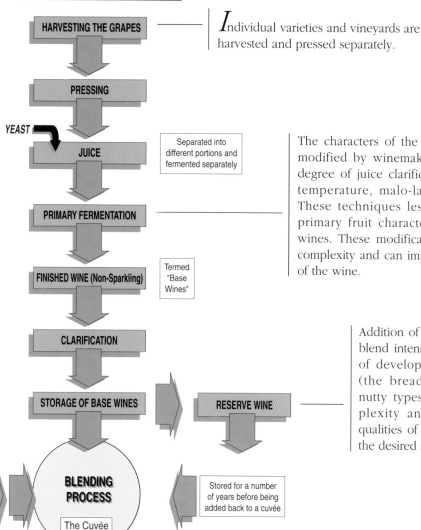

HARVESTING THE GRAPES — *I*ndividual varieties and vineyards are harvested and pressed separately.

PRESSING

YEAST → **JUICE** — Separated into different portions and fermented separately

PRIMARY FERMENTATION

The characters of the base wines can be modified by winemaking techniques eg, degree of juice clarification, fermentation temperature, malo-lactic fermentation. These techniques lessen the impact of primary fruit characters in the finished wines. These modifications add a further complexity and can improve the mouthfeel of the wine.

FINISHED WINE (Non-Sparkling) — Termed "Base Wines"

CLARIFICATION

Addition of reserve wine to the blend intensifies the expression of developed fruit characters (the bready, toasty, honey, nutty types), increasing complexity and fine-tuning the qualities of the cuvée to match the desired style.

STORAGE OF BASE WINES → **RESERVE WINE**

BLENDING PROCESS

The Cuvée

Base wines from different varieties, vineyards and years are blended to produce the desired style of sparkling wine

Stored for a number of years before being added back to a cuvée

Yeast and sugar are added to the blended wine which is then divided into individual bottles where the secondary fermentation occurs

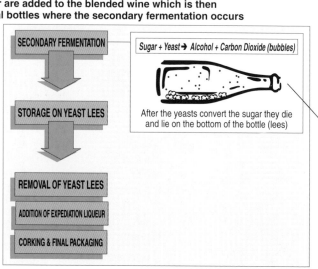

SECONDARY FERMENTATION

Sugar + Yeast → Alcohol + Carbon Dioxide (bubbles)

After the yeasts convert the sugar they die and lie on the bottom of the bottle (lees)

During this period (which may be from 9 months up to 5 years) the dead yeast releases compounds into the wine, and, as well, components of the base wine are modified as the wine ages. These two processes contribute new bouquet and flavour sensations to the wine

STORAGE ON YEAST LEES

REMOVAL OF YEAST LEES

ADDITION OF EXPEDIATION LIQUEUR

CORKING & FINAL PACKAGING

mousse

bead

This gives the wine its bubbles.

Bubbles should be small and form a persistent bead and mousse.

The alcohol level of these wines is about 12% alcohol by volume.

SENSORY FEATURES OF SPARKLING WINES

APPEARANCE

The colour of sparkling wine can vary from pale straw through to deep yellow. Rosé styles are coloured light red. The bubbles should be small and form a persistent bead and mousse.

AROMAS AND FLAVOURS

Often the features of these wines are their subtlety. Their characters are not as immediately obvious as in some other table wines.

Generally, the aromas and flavours present in sparkling wine are a mix of primary fruit, wine-making induced and developed characters. However, the contribution of each feature may vary in any particular wine. Some sparkling wines show more obvious primary fruit characters. In other sparkling wines delicate primary fruit sensations intermingle with subtle developed characters that come from age and yeast autolysis.

In other wines the developed characters can be more intense. We describe some of these different characters on page 66.

THE PALATE

Fine sparkling wine can invoke a feeling of lightness and delicacy in the mouth. Palate structure is important. As well as showing an intensity of subtle flavours, the palate should be complex and have length and persistency. A pleasant creamy feeling in the mouth should complement the crisp, drying acidity.

Sparkling wine styles

Sparkling wines vary in style from the so-called 'apéritif' style through to fuller, developed styles.

The 'apéritif' style is more delicately flavoured and structured. Subtle primary fruit characters are finely balanced with developed characters. The finish should be crisp and fresh. These wines, although more delicate and lighter bodied, can still be complex and have a creamy mouthfeel. You will remember that we suggested appropriate descriptors for sparkling wine on page 66. Some descriptors for apéritif style wines are likely to be *green apple, grapefruit, lemon, biscuity, bready, toasty* and *honey*. These wines are predominantly Chardonnay based.

The fuller bodied styles have a greater impact in the mouth, with more powerful and rich flavours and often with less emphasis on primary fruit characters. They can also have a soft, creamy mouthfeel. Some descriptors for these styles include *meaty, cold lamb, bready, toasty, nutty, honey* and *mushroom*. These wines are normally a blend of Chardonnay and Pinot Noir with Pinot Noir making up the major proportion. The quality of each of the above styles depends very much on the intensity of the various flavours and their balance with the weight and structure of the wine on the palate.

Consumer choice for any particular style varies considerably and depends on personal preference, the food that accompanies the wine and the occasion.

Some producers to choose from include Petaluma, Yalumba, Peter Rumball, Orlando, Wolf Blass Wines, Hardys, Andrew Garrett and Mountadam in South Australia; Chateau Remy, Taltarni, Cope-Williams, Hanging Rock, Yellowglen, Seppelt, Brown Brothers and Domaine Chandon in Victoria; and Heemskerk in Tasmania.

Hanging Rock Winery is in the Macedon region of Victoria.

Chateau Remy Winery is in the Pyrenees region of Victoria.

Australian producers of sparkling wine have only just commenced their journey towards style definition. Regions such as the Adelaide Hills in South Australia, the foothills of the alps in New South Wales and Victoria, the Macedon region of Victoria and parts of Tasmania are now the source of grapes for many premium sparkling wines. Grapes are being sourced from these newer, cooler climate vineyards, experience is being gained with winemaking techniques and blending, and stocks of reserve wines are being accumulated; all of these will contribute to even better Australian sparkling wines in the future.

A tasting experience

SEAVIEW BRUT

SEAVIEW PINOT CHARDONNAY

EDWARDS & CHAFFEY

T H E   G R A P E S

The wine is predominantly a blend of Pinot Noir and Chardonnay with some Muscadelle, Chenin Blanc and Semillon wines from vineyards in cool to warm regions.

A blend of only Pinot Noir and Chardonnay. The fruit is sourced from premium cool climate sites.

A blend of only premium Pinot Noir and Chardonnay, which are sourced mainly from high altitude, cold climate vineyard sites in the Snowy Mountains of New South Wales and Victoria and the Adelaide Hills.

T H E   W I N E M A K I N G

This is a Non Vintage wine. Reserve wine has been added to the blend before secondary fermentation. Most of the base wines undergo a malo-lactic fermentation. The wine is matured on yeast lees for up to twelve months.

This is a Vintage wine with Pinot Noir being a major proportion of the blend. The base wines undergo a malo-lactic fermentation. The wine spends from two to three years maturing on yeast lees.

This is a Vintage wine. The cuvée is made up of mainly Pinot Noir base wines. Malo-lactic fermentation adds complexity to the base wines. Skilful selection of the finest of vintage base wines produces a cuvée with great potential for ageing on yeast lees. The wine is aged on yeast lees for three or more years.

T H E   T A S T E   O F   T H E   W I N E

The wine is pale/lemon gold, with a steady bead of bubbles. The bouquet is fresh and inviting, showing lifted fruit characters (often apple and melon) enhanced with subtle yeastiness. On the palate the wine is flavoursome and has a refreshing dry finish. A full, mouthfilling wine with a soft, creamy texture.

The wine is straw in colour with a fine, persistent bead. The bouquet is complex, with Pinot Noir primary fruit characters mingling with biscuity, bready characters from development on yeast lees. Some malo-lactic characters may be evident. The palate is complex and flavoursome with soft and creamy texture and length of flavour balanced with crisp acidity. An elegant, flavoursome and complex wine.

The wine is straw-gold in colour with a fine, persistent bead and mousse. A rich, complex bouquet with a touch of Pinot Noir primary fruit characters, but mainly complex developed features of cold lamb, crushed biscuits and some nuttiness. The palate shows great depth, creaminess and complexity of flavours, elegant structure and a soft, dry, lingering finish.

Quality, reliable and affordable.

A crafted quality product, select grapes and skilful winemaking.

Premium quality, the pursuit of excellence.

We have focused on the Méthode Champenoise process since it is the most exciting part of the Australian sparkling wine industry and these wines highlight the quality and potential that can be expected from premium Australian sparkling wine. These wines may often seem expensive but they are costly to produce and they do represent the best from each producer.

However, as for other wine styles, each producer may make a range of wines of different qualities and price points. The less expensive wines also offer rewarding tastes. They generally show a greater emphasis on primary fruit characters and have less complexity of flavour and mouthfeel. They may be made by either the Méthode Champenoise or the transfer method.

Some examples to try: Orlando Carrington, Seppelt Great Western, Seaview Brut, Yalumba Angus Brut, Penfolds Minchinbury, De Bortoli Jean Pierre.

What you will see on the label

The word Champagne rightly belongs to those wines produced in the Champagne region of France.

Some Australian sparkling wines still have the word Champagne on the label, but this is changing with time.

The distinction in style and quality between Vintage and Non Vintage is not clearly established in Australia, as it is in Champagne. This will evolve though, as producers develop their 'house styles' and as they increase the amount of reserve wines in their cellars. Australian producers are now developing special names for their sparkling wines and, with time, consumers will come to appreciate the style and quality of wine associated with each of these names.

Apéritif styles go well with appetizers and seafood. The fuller bodied styles can accompany a range of food including hors d'oeuvres, seafood, chicken, game and light meat dishes prepared with delicate sauces and also with light desserts.

Enjoying sparkling wine

Preparing for the occasion

Sparkling wine is best served chilled. Place the bottle in the fridge a couple of hours before serving, or in an ice filled bucket about half an hour before serving.

Opening the bottle

Tilt the bottle away from yourself and other people. Untwist the wire muselet, loosen it and remove it. Hold the cork firmly with one hand and twist the bottle with the other. Allow the cork to come out gently by applying downward pressure on the cork as it slowly comes out of the bottle.

Serving the wine

Sparkling wine is best served in a tall, narrow flute. Pour a little wine into the glass, wait a moment for the effervescence to subside and then pour more wine into the glass. Never completely fill the flute. Allow some space so that the subtle fragrances can fill the top of the flute, enhancing the enjoyment of the delicate bouquet.

DOMAINE

CHANDON

1992 BRUT

750ML PRODUCE OF AUSTRALIA

YALUMBA

Méthode Champenoise   Vintage 1991

YALUMBA WINERY EDEN VALLEY ROAD ANGASTON SOUTH AUSTRALIA 5353
750ML PRODUCE OF AUSTRALIA

SEPPELT

SALINGER

Méthode Champenoise
Vintage 1990

750ML

Some
**of Australia's
well-established
premium sparkling wines.**

VINTAGE
1991
RANDALL
SAUVAGE

PINOT NOIR / CHARDONNAY

750ML

METHODE

CHAMPENOISE

YELLOWGLEN

Home & Landragin

METHODE CHAMPENOISE
WINE PRODUCE OF AUSTRALIA   750ML

1992

CROSER

ALCOHOL 12.5%   WINE MADE IN AUSTRALIA   750ML

There is nothing quite like the crimson red, almost plasma-coloured, 'alive' mousse of a young Sparkling Burgundy. However, the appeal of these wines lies not with the bubbles, but with the complexity they develop with age.

If Australia were to lay claim to three unique, internationally accepted wine styles, they would be Aged Hunter Valley Semillon, Muscat of Rutherglen and **Sparkling Burgundy**.

The term 'Sparkling Burgundy' is used to describe a red wine that has undergone a secondary yeast fermentation in the bottle, giving it bubbles. The process is similar to the Méthode Champenoise but the sparkling wine produced is deep red in colour and has distinctly different tastes to other sparkling wines.

Sparkling Burgundy was first produced from Pinot Noir grapes in Burgundy, France in 1820. In 1881 Sparkling Burgundy was first made in Australia, also from Pinot Noir wine. Then in 1893, Edmond Mazure made a Sparkling Burgundy style wine using Shiraz base wines at the Auldana winery near Adelaide, a wine that was intensely crimson red and richly flavoured. This wine was vastly different to the Pinot Noir based wines. The style of sparkling wines produced from Shiraz base wines became known as Australian Sparkling Burgundy.

How traditional Australian Sparkling Burgundy wines are made

The grapes
Shiraz grapes, preferably with intense plum, blackberry, and licorice aromas and flavours, are used to produce this style. Each batch of grapes is harvested and processed into a dry red wine. Fermentation techniques that give good flavour and colour extraction but avoid excessive tannin extraction are normally used (cooler fermentations and gentle extraction).

The blending
After all the wines are made they are tasted and those with the right characters (normally rich flavours but soft tannins) are selected as base wines.

Non vintage styles
The cuvée is made up of young and older base wines. The older base wines may have been stored in large vats or older barrels, or even in bottles, for a number of years before they are selected. They contribute aged characters to the cuvée.

Vintage styles
The very best base wines from a particular year are used to prepare the cuvée.

Secondary fermentation (Méthode Champenoise)
After the composition of the cuvée is decided, the selected wines are mixed with an amount of sugar and yeast and then transferred to heavyweight pressure-tested bottles. These are the bottles in which the secondary fermentation will take place and in which the wine will be sold.

Most commercial styles remain on yeast lees for one to three years. Others, such as Seppelt Show Sparkling Burgundy, may spend seven or more years on yeast lees. During this time, the yeast autolysis characters merge with those of maturing fruit to give complexity and creamy tactile sensations develop. When it is decided that the wine has spent sufficient time on yeast lees, the processes of remuage, disgorging, dosage, bottling and packaging take place.

At the dosage stage a sugar solution may be added to balance the astringency of the wine. The level of sugar addition may range from about 8 to about 40 grams per litre of residual sugar. Also at this stage there is opportunity to add a touch of either older or younger wine to fine-tune the taste of the finished product.

Bottle maturation ('time on cork')
Some time is usually necessary for the dosage additions to blend harmoniously with the wine. Some wines will be left to mature in the bottle to take on more developed characters before they are released.

Usually the longer the time on cork, the less the gas pressure within the bottle. Classic older examples (some of which may be wax sealed) frequently open without a 'pop', providing only a tingling tactile sensation on the tongue as a reminder of an earlier sparkling past. The wine, however, is usually well preserved, soft, generous and often with a velvet-like texture.

SENSORY FEATURES OF TRADITIONAL AUSTRALIAN SPARKLING BURGUNDY

APPEARANCE

Colours of young wines are deep, crimson red. They should have a fine persistent bead, forming a strong, crimson red mousse.

Older wines may be garnet red with ruby hues grading to leather brown.

AROMAS AND FLAVOURS

Primary fruit characters include *spice, pepper, cherry, violet, plum, plum pudding, mulberry, blackberry, licorice, sarsaparilla* and *jammy.*

Developed fruit characters include *earthy, sweet, barnyard, slight leathery, mushrooms, truffles, meaty, smoky* and *chocolate.*

THE PALATE

The palate should be rich, full-flavoured and complex, have soft tannins and length of sweet berry fruit characters. The finish should be dry and not overly astringent.

Older wines, and particularly those that have had extensive yeast lees contact, will show greater complexity and a creamy, velvety mouth-feel.

A tasting experience

Some examples to try:

Seppelt
Rockford
Peter Rumball
Craneford
Brown Brothers
Charles Melton
Barossa Valley Estates
Hardys

What you will see on the label

With time, the term 'Sparkling Burgundy' will disappear from Australian wine labels.
What will replace it?
Some will be labelled 'Sparkling Shiraz' and others by brand names, but perhaps someone will invent a new, innovative name for this unique style of Australian wine.

Other sparkling red wines

Other black grape varieties such as Pinot Noir, Cabernet Sauvignon, Merlot and Durif can also be made into sparkling red wines. These may be made by the Méthode Champenoise process or by any of the other methods for making sparkling wine.

The aromas, flavours and taste sensations of these wines depend very much on what primary fruit characters were present in the grapes at harvest, how long the base wines were aged and how long the wine was stored on yeast lees.

Some of these wines, as well as some sparkling Shiraz wines, may show oak influence, but fruit flavours (either primary or developed) and not oak should be the feature of these wines.

These wines offer a choice in sparkling red wine styles, and many give rich, flavoursome tastes, but the flavours are different from those of sparkling wines made from Shiraz-based wines.

Some examples to try:

Yalumba Cuvée Prestige Cabernet Sauvignon
Jim Irvine Sparkling Merlot Brut
Mick Morris Sparkling Shiraz Durif
Brand's Laira Sparkling Coonawarra

These Seppelt Show Sparkling Burgundies offer complex bouquet and flavours; spice, pepper and plum flavours of youth in harmony with the earthy and other characters of age. The long time that these wines spend on yeast lees provides further complexity and texture to the palate. These are wines that epitomize the taste of classic Australian Sparkling Burgundy.

Some of these Show Sparkling Burgundies can age magnificently in the bottle for many years.

Sparkling Burgundy is the perfect accompaniment for turkey, duck, kangaroo and strong cheeses.

Orlando's Jacob's Creek Vineyard in the Barossa Valley.

*D*ry white table wine

Australian winemakers have led the way in the application of technology to the making of white wines. The use of refrigeration, clarification of juice prior to fermentation and careful selection of yeast have all contributed to ensuring that these wines are full of distinctive characters. They are wines full of aromas and flavours that remind the taster of the grape varieties from which the wines were made. Furthermore, the widescale adoption of traditional methods in the making of Chardonnay and other medium- to full-bodied white wines produces wines which have not only abundant, distinctive and diverse flavours, but also great complexity, structure and mouthfeel.

Wines from the varieties Riesling, Gewürztraminer and Sauvignon Blanc are normally light- to medium-bodied, exhibiting predominantly primary fruit aromas and flavours. They are dry, crisp and refreshing to taste. Most are 'early drinking' styles, but if you cellar some of our Rieslings you will be amply rewarded for your patience, as they develop intriguing complexity with time.

Wines from the varieties Chardonnay, Semillon and Marsanne are normally medium- to full-bodied styles, with more complex aromas and flavours and alluring tactile sensations. Many of these wines get better with age. The complexity and textural sensations that come from techniques such as barrel fermentation and malo-lactic fermentation bring mouthfeel and interest to the taste and enjoyment of these wines. Many Australian Chardonnay wines show such features. However, we are only beginning to explore these techniques for other white wine grape varieties, making wines with layers of flavours and mouthfeel sensations. If you are a red wine lover, try some of Australia's multi-flavoured and textured white wines; their tastes can be as enjoyable and fascinating as those of red wines.

The future of Australian white wines is exciting. Enjoy their tastes. You will find them to be generously flavoured and often with marked differences due to variety, region and maker.

Riesling

Riesling (or Rhine Riesling as it is sometimes called) is regarded as one of the world's great white wine grape varieties. It is the main variety grown in the Rhine and Mosel Valleys of Germany.

Historically, the word 'Riesling' has been used on labels of Australian wine either to indicate that the wine is a varietal wine made from Riesling grapes, or to describe a generic style of dry white wine. The word Riesling in the latter case indicates that the wine is a light-bodied, dry, fruity white wine, but not necessarily made from Riesling grapes. The use of this form of labelling is less common now and most wines labelled Riesling or Rhine Riesling will be varietal wines.

Wines from the variety Riesling, as well as from other aromatic varieties, are made with meticulous care to protect the delicate fruit aromas and flavours of the grape. They are made from highly clarified juice, fermented at low temperatures and protected from oxidation throughout their making. They do not undergo malo-lactic fermentation and are not stored in oak barrels; the prime concern of the winemaker is to maintain freshness and intensity of primary fruit characters balanced with a crisp acid taste.

SENSORY FEATURES OF RIESLING WINES

APPEARANCE

The colour of young wines can range from straw through to light yellow, often with green tinges. With age the wines take on deeper yellow colours.

AROMAS AND FLAVOURS
Primary fruit characters

The aromas and flavours of Riesling wines are often described as:
floral, fragrant, perfumed, rose-petal, cold tea, pear, lemon, citrus, lime, grapefruit, pineapple, fruity, passionfruit and *tropical fruit.*

Developed fruit characters

The best of our Rieslings, particularly those with high acid and fruit intensity when young, develop wonderful *toasty, honey-like* characters as they age. Sometimes, a *kerosene* character can develop; this can add some complexity, but it is

pleasing only if present in small amounts. These intriguing tastes of bottle-aged Riesling harmonise with the youthful floral, citrus, limey flavours and add further dimensions to the enjoyment of our Riesling wines. Regrettably, too many of our Rieslings are consumed when they are young.

THE PALATE

Australian dry Riesling styles are light- to medium-bodied wines, but generally have more palate weight than many of their European counterparts. They are normally made from ripe grapes, both sugar and flavour ripe, providing wines with a full middle palate, delicious fruit, lingering aftertastes and a crisp, acid finish.

The sugar content may vary from about 2 to around 7 grams per litre. Wines with sugar content towards the higher end of this range may taste slightly sweet, but most of our Rieslings are bone dry, containing only a few grams of sugar per litre. Winemakers will balance the sugar and acid levels of any wine so that they are in harmony with each other and with the flavour intensity of the wine.

Grapes grown in warmer sites develop less of the floral, fragrant characters, but can still have intense citrus, lime, and some tropical fruit-like characters. The cooler the climatic conditions under which the grapes ripen, the greater the intensity of floral, fragrant, citrus (lemon) characters and the more naturally acidic the wine may taste. These wines give a sensation on the palate that is often described as 'steely'; it relates to the crispness of the acid and associated structural features.

Riesling grapes can be made into either dry, semi-sweet or sweet white wine styles; we discuss the sweeter styles in the next chapter.

A tasting experience

| **JACOB'S CREEK RHINE RIESLING** | **ST HELGA EDEN VALLEY RHINE RIESLING** | **STEINGARTEN RHINE RIESLING** |

T H E   G R A P E S

Grapes are sourced from over 30 separate vineyards in the Barossa, the Southern Vales, Coonawarra, Mildura, Clare and Padthaway districts. A large percentage of the grapes normally comes from the Barossa Valley.

Prior to harvest the winemakers identify select vineyards or sections of vineyards in the Eden Valley region in the elevated ranges above the Barossa Valley. Eden Valley is renowned for producing grapes of high acid and intensity of elegant fruit characters. The grapes are harvested at optimum ripeness.

In 1962, Orlando set up a prestige Rhine Riesling vineyard to emulate the conditions often found in the famous German vineyards: high altitude, shallow well-drained soils and close vine planting. The vineyard, planted on a steep ridge high in the Barossa Hills, was called Steingarten.

T H E   W I N E M A K I N G

After crushing, the must is chilled to 8°C and held on skins for a short time. The free run juice is then drained and cold settled. Some light pressings are added prior to fermentation, which is conducted at cool temperatures.

The vineyards are harvested at night, and the juice is taken off skins quickly and then fermented cool to retain the intensity of delicate fruit flavours. After fermentation, wines from each vineyard are tasted and the best selected to go into the St Helga blend.

The grapes are hand harvested. The juice is meticulously cared for and then fermented cool to retain and highlight the fine, delicate flavours and structure which are the hallmark of this single vineyard wine.

T H E   T A S T E   O F   T H E   W I N E

The wine is normally straw to light yellow coloured. Expect to experience attractive fresh lime/citrus fruit characters on the nose and palate, balanced by a crisp, acid finish. This is a wine to be enjoyed when it is young.

The colour typically is pale straw green. The taste exemplifies the style of wine that comes from Eden Valley: delicately scented, floral tones intermingled with fresh lemon, lime aromas and flavours, balanced with fresh acidity. This elegant, intensely flavoured, high acid style of Riesling can be enjoyed in its youth, but has the propensity to improve with age, developing lovely toasty, honey complexity.

It is normally pale straw green in colour, a wine that has an enviable reputation, displaying intensity of elegant floral, grapefruit and lime characters. A feature is the great length of fine flavours, and a structure on the palate that gives a crisp, flinty, steely finish, characteristic of cool climate Riesling. This is a classic wine, which with time takes on toasty, honey complexity and offers excellent cellaring potential.

Quality, reliable and affordable.

A crafted quality product, select grapes and skilful winemaking.

Premium quality, the pursuit of excellence.

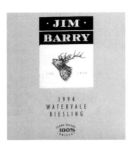

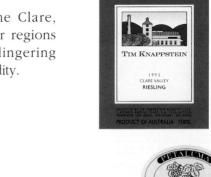

*T*ypically, Rieslings from the Clare, Watervale and Polish Hill River regions have citrus/lime characters, lingering flavours and refreshing crisp acidity.

● **CLARE**

The Clare Region

The Polish Hill River Region

SEVENHILL ●

The Watervale Region

● **WATERVALE**

AUBURN ○

ADELAIDE ↓ (130km)

total flavour

Flavour

cedar wood

tropical fruit

steely

citrus (limes)

honey

1 year 2 years 3 years 4 years 5 years

∧
Vintage

This is how John Wilson (winemaker of The Wilson Vineyard, Polish Hill River region of South Australia) describes changes in his Rhine Rieslings with time.

'Typically these wines emerge from vintage with citric flavour (predominantly limes) and a steely backbone. Very quickly they acquire flavours of tropical fruit (passionfruit, pineapples, monstera fruit), and reach a peak between one and two years old. The steeliness starts to fade early, and by two years the fresh tropical flavours are declining. There seems to be no change in the apparent level of citrus flavour over time.

With age a honeyed character emerges, although it appears that the intensity of this may be related to the sugar content of the wine, and possibly the level of ripeness at which the grapes were picked.

Later still, there appear cedar-wood characters. Bear in mind that these wines have no wood contact at all.'

John Wilson

Part of enjoying wine is tasting wines from different regions. Try this selection and experience the tastes of some of Australia's fine Riesling wines.

The Eden Valley and the Clare Valley are renowned for their Riesling wines. With the expansion of vineyards into new cool regions, the choice of fine Riesling wines is now even greater.

A Selection Of Australian Rieslings

South Australia

Western Australia

Great Southern
Howard Park
Plantagenet
Jingalla
Goundrey
Alkoomi

Margaret River
Leeuwin

Australind
Capel Vale

Clare Valley
There are many producers in the regions around Clare. Also a number of other producers source fruit from these regions including Petaluma, Wolf Blass Wines and Wirra Wirra.

Eden Valley
Mountadam
Craneford
Many producers source fruit from this region, including Wolf Blass Wines, Orlando, Leo Buring, Tollana, Henschke, Peter Lehmann, Grant Burge, Yalumba, and Chapel Hill

Adelaide Hills
Glenara
Ashton Hills

McLaren Vale
Wirra Wirra
Chapel Hill

Padthaway/Coonawarra
Wynns
Leconfield
Katnook

Victoria

Macedon
Knights

Goulburn Valley
Mitchelton
Chateau Tahbilk

Victorian High Country
Delatite
Plunkett

New South Wales

Canberra District
Clonakilla
Doonkuna Estate

Tasmania

North East
Pipers Brook
Heemskerk

South East
Fishburn and O'Keefe
Moorilla
Elsewhere Vineyard

Moorilla Estate's winery and restaurant complex is located just north of Hobart.

Enjoy Riesling with shellfish, oysters, fish and poultry.

Gewürztraminer

You will also see this wine labelled as Traminer. It is probably the most easily recognised varietal wine; its *primary fruit characters* are very distinct and descriptors include *floral, spicy, perfumed, roses, limes, lychees* and *lavender.*

These fragrant aromas and flavours are balanced with crisp acidity. The wines are light- to medium-bodied and are generally 'early drinking' styles, and are an excellent accompaniment to seafood, asparagus and Chinese and Thai food.

One of the best examples of this type is from Tolley in South Australia.

The fruit is sourced from their 'Pedare' vineyards in the Barossa Valley and consistently produces wines with spicy, perfumed and limey aromas and flavours, full flavoured palate, crisp acid finish and long aftertaste. It is a great match with Chinese food.

The spicy, perfumed and lychee characters are most evident when the grapes develop in cool climatic conditions.

Other examples of wines from this variety include:

Orlando Flaxman's Eden Valley Traminer from South Australia;

Brown Brothers Gewürztraminer from King Valley in Victoria;

Idyll Vineyard Classic Dry Gewürztraminer from the Geelong region in Victoria;

Delatite Winery Gewürztraminer from the High Country in Victoria; and

Moorilla Estate Gewürztraminer from Tasmania.

Traminer/Riesling blends

Many wines are derived from blends of these two varieties. They may be dry styles, but more often they are made into slightly sweeter styles, to provide more fullness on the palate.

Frontignac

Frontignac is another variety that can produce intensely fragrant, perfumed wines. It can be made into either dry or sweet styles of white wine.

Sauvignon Blanc

This is a variety that produces light- to medium-bodied wines. They are made from clear juice, fermented at low temperature (about 10°C) and protected from oxidation to retain the delicate varietal aromas and flavours. They can be made in many different styles, often reflecting the climatic and viticultural conditions in which the grapes have developed.

Vines which have dense canopies (where the bunches of grapes and inside leaves are shaded by outer leaves) can produce grapes and wines with high levels of methoxy pyrazine, a compound that has intense asparagus, canned green peas or capsicum-like characters. These characters intensify even more when such vines are grown in very cool environments. Generally, most grapegrowers and winemakers strive to keep these characters in check, a challenge which starts in the vineyard. Improving the trellis and spreading the vine's canopy, or removing leaves in the vicinity of the bunches, exposes the leaves and bunches to more sunlight. Under these improved light conditions the ripening pattern of the grapes is modified so that the methoxy pyrazine-like tones are lessened while the gooseberry and tropical fruit characters are enhanced. Wines made from grapes such as these tend also to have a fuller palate.

The *varietal characters* of Sauvignon Blanc wines depend on where and how the grapes were grown and are often described as *vegetal, asparagus, capsicum, tomato bush, freshly cut grass, grassy, gooseberry, passionfruit, melons* and *tropical fruit.*

Good wines generally have a well balanced mixture of herbaceous, grassy, gooseberry and tropical fruit nuances, but often with intense fresh gooseberry tones predominating. A touch of herbaceous, asparagus-like aromas and flavours can add extra interest and a lift to the nose of the wine.

These wines are normally light- to medium-bodied and should have a fresh, crisp finish and a long aftertaste. Some may be more full-bodied, since apart from the variations in aroma and flavours that come from the vineyard, winemaking practice can also influence the sensory features of these wines. Further differences can evolve if the wine is stored in oak barrels.

SENSORY FEATURES OF SAUVIGNON BLANC WINES

APPEARANCE
The colour of these wines ranges from straw to yellow.

AROMAS, FLAVOURS AND PALATE SENSATIONS

Non-wooded styles
The better wines show an intensity of varietal flavours, normally a mixture of flavours but predominantly grassy, gooseberry accents, long aftertaste and a fresh crisp finish. The presence of excessive asparagus and canned green pea types of characters may be unpleasant in some wines, often being described as 'over the top'. It is very much a matter of personal preference whether the degree to which these characters are present in any particular wine is perceived as an enjoyable feature.

Sauvignon Blanc wines are usually enjoyed as fresh young wines and most have only a short to medium ageing potential (a few years).

Wooded styles
Winemakers often make different batches of wines from different vineyards or different sections of the one vineyard. Some of the wines are totally fermented and stored in stainless steel, while others may be stored in oak barrels for a number of months. Other techniques such as barrel fermentation and time on yeast lees may also be employed in their making.

The wines are then assessed prior to blending and the winemakers decide on the various proportions of non-wooded and wooded wines to make up the blend. As a rule, they will be looking for a consistent style from year to year. The wine is often labelled 'Fumé Blanc'. This name was devised by Robert Mondavi of Mondavi Wines in California to indicate a wood-matured Sauvignon Blanc. These wines, as well as having varietal Sauvignon Blanc characters, will show restrained smoky oak aromas and flavours, giving some complexity and more variation to the smell and taste of the wine. The palate will have more weight, and generally they will be more medium-bodied wines. The finish of these wines should be fresh and dry.

Blended styles
In other instances, wines from Sauvignon Blanc are blended with wines of other varieties, typically Semillon, and can be wooded or unwooded. Semillon contributes extra flavours and tends to give a fuller palate to these blended styles. Sometimes these blends are also labelled 'Fumé Blanc'. In Margaret River, they are often labelled 'Classic Dry White'.

Look for gooseberry fruit with touches of grass and herbs, middle palate fullness, length and a crisp dry finish.

Stafford Ridge is located at Lenswood in the Adelaide Hills of South Australia.

Shaw and Smith is also in the Adelaide Hills region.

You will find Yarra Ridge in the Yarra Valley of Victoria.

Katnook is located in the Coonawarra region of South Australia.

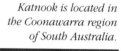

These wines will show distinctive varietal fruit characters with subtle oak integration.

Tim Knappstein of Clare in South Australia and Taltarni in the Pyrenees region of Victoria pioneered the 'Fumé Blanc' styles in Australia.

Try Sauvignon Blanc wines with oysters, smoked salmon, fresh asparagus, chicken or a plate of antipasto.

Semillon

Semillon is a white wine grape variety that can be made into many styles.

SENSORY FEATURES OF SEMILLON WINES

APPEARANCE
The wines will range in colour from straw to yellow.

AROMAS, FLAVOURS AND PALATE SENSATIONS

Primary fruit characters include
herbaceous, pea-pod, green, grassy, flinty, straw, gooseberry, apple, quince, lemon, lime, citrus, fig, and *tropical fruit.*

Grapes and wines from cooler regions are more likely to have lively herbaceous, pea-pod, grassy tones coupled with lemon and citrus characters, while those from warmer regions will usually have less herbaceousness and a greater intensity of lemon and citrus characters as well as some tropical fruit nuances.

But again, winemaking influence can modify the style of the wine. Generally we can categorise the styles as follows:

Non-wooded styles
These are styles, normally from cooler regions, in which the fresh, vibrant, herbaceous, grassy, citrus varietal characters dominate the nose and palate and are balanced with crisp acidity. Often Semillon wines from the Margaret River region of Western Australia are made in this style, although a number may show some subtle oak characters.

Some producers from Western Australia include:

Evans and Tate
Sandalford
Chateau Xanadu
Killerby
Moss Wood

Wooded styles
These are fuller bodied styles (often from warmer climates) which may show some herbaceousness but mainly lemon and tropical fruit-like aromas and flavours. Generally they have been aged in wood. They show various degrees of vanillin and other oak characters. Further complexity can be moulded into these wooded styles through barrel fermentation, time on lees and malo-lactic fermentation. These techniques may add creamy, buttery, nutty tones to the nose and palate, as well as contributing texture to the palate. These are wines that are best described as having layers of flavours.

Variations of these Semillon styles can be found in all our wine regions, from Stanthorpe in Queensland through to Margaret River in Western Australia.

Some examples to try include these Semillons from:
(the degree of oak influence will vary between wines from the different producers)

Queensland
Ballandean Estate
Winewood

Victoria
Shantell
Hickinbotham
Bannockburn
Mount Avoca

New South Wales
Miramar
Rosemount
Cassegrain

South Australia
Grant Burge
Peter Lehmann
Basedow
Bethany
Rockford
Penfolds
Grossett
Tim Adams
Coriole

Barossa Valley Semillons often show greater oak influence, but this is generally well integrated with riper fruit characters.

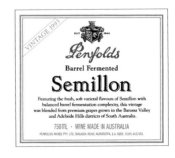

Blended styles

Semillon can be blended with other varieties, often Sauvignon Blanc or Chardonnay. You will find these blended styles from many of our wine regions.

Classic Hunter Valley aged Semillon styles

Some Hunter Valley producers are releasing styles similar to those described previously, but the Hunter Valley is better known for developed, bottle aged Semillons. It is rare today for wine companies to age wine in the bottle prior to release, but this is exactly what happens with aged Hunter Semillons. The fruit is picked at relatively low sugar levels (10-11° Baumé). The best years are when the grapes are naturally high in acid. The grapes are crushed and the clear juice (often with the pressing component added) is fermented cool (10-12°C). After fermentation the wine is clarified, filtered and bottled. These wines do not undergo malo-lactic fermentation and are not stored in oak barrels. The wines are then aged in the bottle for up to six years (or longer) before they are released onto the market. They can continue to improve in the bottle for many years. Some of these wines are still magnificent twenty years or more after they are bottled.

When bottled, these wines are light straw in colour and may appear quite neutral, having light grassy, apple and lemon-like aromas and flavours. The characters of these wines gradually change as they age in the bottle. With time these subtly flavoured wines develop deep golden colours, build in weight and take on variations of *rich toasty, honey, fig* developed characters. This interesting complexity coupled with relatively low alcohol content (about 11%v/v), is the trademark of this style of wine. An added advantage is that they are relatively inexpensive to buy as younger wines.

Enjoy Semillon with seafood, chicken, veal, pasta dishes and game, depending on the style of the wine.

Semillons can also be made into sweet white wine styles, which we cover in the next chapter.

A Collection Of Classic Hunter Valley Semillons

Colombard

This is a white wine grape variety that performs well in warmer climates, since at ripeness the grapes can have high acid content as well as good flavours. Its *varietal descriptors* include: *herbaceous, grassy, apple, citrus, lime, melon, passionfruit, tropical fruit* and *honeysuckle.*

Some good examples may be obtained from Primo Estate Wines in the Adelaide Plains Region and Angove's in the Riverland Region of South Australia.

Chenin Blanc

This is a grape variety that produces crisp, flavoursome white wines. *Varietal descriptors* include: *herbaceous, herbal, grassy, floral, sweaty* and *honey.*

Often the wines are stored in wood. They may be labelled as Chablis, a term we discuss on page 88.

Some Chenin Blanc examples to try:

Houghton in Western Australia

Henschke in South Australia

Broken River Wines in Victoria use Chenin Blanc to produce a still wine and also a sparkling wine style by the Méthode Champenoise process.

Verdelho

Verdelho is a Portuguese variety. In Australia it is used to produce dry, sweet and fortified wine styles. It performs well in a range of climates and is gaining in popularity, this being reflected in the increased plantings over recent years. Western Australia and the Hunter Valley have been the main areas where this variety has been grown, but it is now expanding into areas such as Cowra in New South Wales.

Its *varietal characters* range from *herbaceous, spicy* and *grassy* through to *melon, pineapple, guava, honeysuckle, tropical fruit* and *fruit salad,* depending on where it is grown and at what stage the grapes are harvested.

Verdelho is best described as a generously flavoured style, reminiscent of tropical fruits, and balanced with crisp acidity. Wines from Verdelho are often quite high in alcohol (about 13-14 %v/v) since the grapes are often picked at the later stages of maturity when they have developed these strong, tropical fruit aromas and flavours. Some of these wines may have been fermented or stored in wood.

Some Verdelho wines to try:

Western Australia

Houghton, Westfield, Sandalford, Happ's, Willespie and Olive Farm. Happ's is a small family winery in the Margaret River region and produces a varietal Verdelho and a blended style with Semillon.

South Australia

Bleasdale at Langhorne Creek makes both a table wine and a fortified sweet wine style.
Sevenhill at Clare produces a blended Verdelho (with Crouchen and Chenin Blanc) labelled as St Aloysius.

New South Wales

Lindemans and Tulloch from the Hunter Valley.
Richmond Grove Cowra Vineyard Verdelho - one of the new Verdelhos on the market.

Marsanne

One of the world's rarest grape varieties, Marsanne is a native of the Côtes du Rhône area in the south of France. Victoria's Goulburn Valley has the second largest plantings of Marsanne in the world. Vines, sourced from St Hubert's vineyards in the Yarra Valley, were established at Chateau Tahbilk in the late 1860s, and although none of the older plantings have survived, the vines that are now used to make Chateau Tahbilk Marsanne are about seventy years old, reputedly the oldest Marsanne vines in the world.

The *primary fruit characters* of Marsanne are described as *lemon, peach* and *honey* but with bottle age these develop into *honeysuckle* fragrances. Generally these wines are medium- to full-bodied with crisp acidity balancing the full array of flavours on the palate.

The Chateau Tahbilk Marsanne is a non-wooded style, typically with characteristic honeysuckle fragrances and crisp acidity.

Mitchelton makes two styles of wine from Marsanne, one a non-wooded, early drinking style under the Thomas Mitchell label, and the other a wood matured, richly flavoured and textured wine labelled Mitchelton Reserve Marsanne.

Mitchelton also produces a wine called Mitchelton III. It is a blend of three Rhône Valley varieties, Marsanne, Grenache and Viognier. This blending of varieties achieves complexity of flavours; further complexity is added through the use of barrel fermentation techniques.

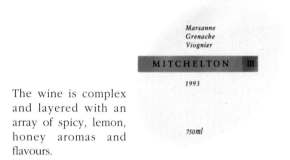

The wine is complex and layered with an array of spicy, lemon, honey aromas and flavours.

Yeringberg, in the Yarra Valley, also produces a Rhône style wine. It is made from a blend of the varieties Marsanne and Roussane and aims to emulate the wines produced at Yeringberg over a hundred years ago.

Viognier

Yalumba has small plantings of Viognier in its Heggies Vineyard. A crisp, dry wine is produced from this variety with citrus characters and subtle oak influence.

Marsanne wines, depending on their style, match a large range of foods from lightly flavoured dishes through to full flavoured poultry, veal, lamb and pork and also cheeses and desserts.

*B*rown Brothers have always had a strong commitment to producing varietal wines. If you plan to set up a varietal tasting, these quality wines from Brown Brothers will be a good introduction. A visit to their cellar door sales facility in Milawa, Victoria offers a great opportunity to try a large range of white and red varietal wines.

Matching wine with food has always been a part of the wine philosophy of Brown Brothers.

Varietal Collection

A classic cool climate style, intense floral, spicy and lime characters on the nose and palate, with a steely acid backbone. Delicious with oysters.

Delicate, spicy and fresh lychee aromas and flavours with a long fresh finish.
A great accompaniment to Thai and Chinese food.

Distinctive and intense musk-like aromas and flavours. A fragrant white wine with refreshing acidity.
A delicious apéritif and a refreshing accompaniment to fish and spicy Asian dishes. This grape variety also produces the rich, flavoursome, sweet wine Spätlese Lexia; we introduce it in the sweet white wine section.

A herbaceous style, elegant fruit flavours with a touch of oak.
A great match for fresh asparagus, seafood and chicken.

Herbaceous, melon, fresh, fruity wine. Match this wine with a wide range of seafood.

Citrus, tropical fruit aromas and flavours and subtle oak influence with a long fresh finish.
A fine partner to seafood or antipasto.

Varietal fruit aromas of citrus, lime, ripe grapefruit and honeysuckle, interwoven with subtle oak and a fine acid finish. A wine showing complexity and layers of flavours.
A good match for highly flavoured fish and chicken dishes.

A wine showing ripe peachy flavours, well integrated with nutty oak characters; rich and complex.
A partner to a wide range of seafood, chicken and pasta dishes and some delicate game dishes.

Chardonnay

This is the white wine grape variety of the Champagne and Burgundy regions of France. It is the most popular white wine grape variety and it is now planted in grape growing regions all around the world. It is grown in all wine regions of Australia, from cool to hot climates, and produces quality wines of vastly different styles across this climatic spectrum. Chardonnay is also a variety where winemakers have many options in crafting the taste of their wines.

What you will see on the label

- Chardonnay
  Indicates a varietal wine.

- Chardonnay/other variety (varieties)
  Chardonnay may be blended with a range of varieties, but most commonly Semillon.

- White Burgundy
  In Australia this term is usually used in the generic sense to indicate a dry, medium- to full-bodied white wine with wood influence and a firm finish. It does not necessarily have to be made from Chardonnay grapes. (In France the term White Burgundy indicates that the wine is made from Chardonnay grapes grown in the Burgundy region.)

  Houghton White Burgundy, a blend of Chardonnay, Verdelho and Chenin Blanc, is one of Australia's most popular White Burgundy styles.

- Chablis
  In Australia this term is used generically to describe a dry white wine with a crisp finish. It does not necessarily have to be made from Chardonnay grapes. (In France the term Chablis indicates that the wine is made from Chardonnay grapes grown in the Chablis region.)

  In time, alternative words will replace the terms White Burgundy and Chablis on bottles of Australian wine.

SENSORY FEATURES OF CHARDONNAY WINES

APPEARANCE

The wines range in colour from straw through to deep yellow depending on where the grapes came from, how the wines were made, and the age of the wine.

AROMAS AND FLAVOURS

Primary fruit characters include
tobacco, apple, grapefruit, lemon, lime, pineapple, melon, rockmelon, fig, peach, tropical fruit, and *fruit salad.*

Wines from grapes grown in cooler climates show predominantly grapefruit, lime, pineapple, melon, and peach-type characters, while those from warm to hot regions are most likely to show more peach, fig, and tropical fruit-like characters. Wines from cool and cool to warm climates normally have a greater intensity of delicate flavours, finer structure and greater longevity.

Developed fruit characters include
toasty, honey, figgy, nutty, cashews.

Characters derived from winemaking

These are additional aromas and flavours that come from barrel fermentation, time on lees, malo-lactic fermentation and barrel storage. They include:

barrel fermentation/time on lees - *creamy, yeasty, vegemite, bonox, marmite, cheesy, bready, toasty* and *leesy;*

malo-lactic fermentation - *creamy, buttery, butterscotch, yogurt* and *caramel;*

barrel fermentation/barrel storage - *vanilla, toasty, sawdust, cedar, olives, spicy, bacon, coconut, pencil shavings, dusty, cashews, smoky, burnt, caramel, raisin* and *charred.*

THE PALATE

Chardonnay wines range from medium- to full-bodied styles. Some may be high in alcohol (often about 13.5%v/v), a feature which contributes to their palate weight. Some wines, particularly those that lack fruit intensity, can be dominated by strong vanillin and resinous characters that come from the oak barrels. The task of the winemaker is to balance the intensity and types of aromas and flavours from the fruit with the characters that come from winemaking techniques, particularly the influence of oak. Australian winemakers are now aiming for more subtle oak integration.

This is how Phillip Shaw, winemaker of Rosemount Estate, describes the role of oak in the making of Roxburgh, Rosemount Estate's prestige Chardonnay wine - 'Oak is used to give the wine extract, not oak character. It gives depth and complexity to the wine and contributes to the richness of flavour'.

Many Chardonnay wines are textured and complex. They can have creamy, cheesy, buttery impressions on the palate. The best wines will have rich, complex, persistent flavours and fine structure, qualities that signal their potential to age magnificently over many years.

Non-wooded styles

These wines focus on the fresh varietal fruit characters of Chardonnay, and are now being produced from a range of climatic regions. The primary fruit characters present in any one wine will very much depend on where the grapes were grown and at what stage of ripeness they were harvested. These non-wooded styles will generally be medium-bodied, highlight the varietal fruit characters and finish fresh and crisp on the palate. They provide a greater choice in the selection and enjoyment of Chardonnay wines, and are labelled as non-wooded or un-wooded Chardonnay.

Some examples to try include:

Mountadam
Chapel Hill
Leconfield
T'Gallant
Shaw and Smith

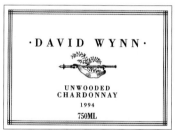

Wooded styles

These represent the styles where winemakers can use their skills to the fullest. They can choose to ferment and/or store the wine in oak barrels, leave the wine on yeast lees, put it through a malo-lactic fermentation or various combinations of these techniques. Often they will make different batches of wine and then blend these to produce the desired style of wine. In this way they can create a symphony of aromas and flavours interwoven with layers of rich and complex taste sensations.

Australia's top selling Chardonnays

Wines made from Chardonnay and/or Chardonnay blends are some of Australia's most well known and popular wines - labels such as Orlando Jacob's Creek, Lindemans Bin 65, Hardys Siegersdorf, Yalumba Oxford Landing, Woodley Queen Adelaide and Houghton White Burgundy. These are wines that generally have plenty of fresh peachy Chardonnay flavours, complemented in many cases by nutty, vanillin, toasty oak characters. You can rely on these wines to be consistent in style. They offer a good taste at an affordable price.

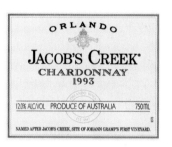

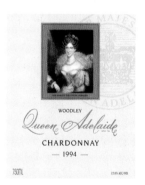

A tasting experience

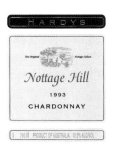  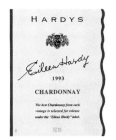

NOTTAGE HILL CHARDONNAY	**CHAIRMANS SELECTION CHARDONNAY**	**EILEEN HARDY CHARDONNAY**

T H E   G R A P E S

Grapes are sourced from a number of regions, including McLaren Vale and Clare, but primarily from the Riverland and Sunraysia regions.

Grapes come from specially selected vineyards in the Riverland region.

Grapes come from prestige cool climate sites: Padthaway in South Australia and Hoddles Creek in Victoria.

T H E   W I N E M A K I N G

After crushing, the must is held on skins for a short time and then pressed. The juice is fermented cool in stainless steel vessels and then stored in oak barrels for a short time.

After crushing and pressing the free run juice is partially fermented in stainless steel tanks and then transferred to new and 1 and 2 year old oak barrels, where the fermentation is completed. Portions of the wine are aged on yeast lees in barrel, others are put through malo-lactic fermentation, while other portions are stored in oak to age for 7 to 9 months. The final wine is a blend of the best of these portions.

After crushing and pressing the free run juice is partially fermented in stainless steel and then transferred to new French oak barrels where the fermentation is completed. The wine is then aged on yeast lees for up to nine months. Approximately 50% of the wine is put through a malo-lactic fermentation to add complexity. The wines from individual barrels are tasted and the best are selected for the Eileen Hardy blend.

T H E   T A S T E   O F   T H E   W I N E

The wine is normally straw to light yellow coloured. Fresh citrus, melon and peachy fruit characters will be balanced with hints of vanillin oak. The palate is soft with medium intensity of flavours. This easy drinking style emphasises fresh fruit characters and is best enjoyed when young.

The colour typically is deep yellow. It is a big, complex style of wine with flavours in the peach, tropical fruit, fruit salad spectrum. Barrel fermentation and malo-lactic fermentation add plenty of creamy, buttery, oaky tones to the nose and palate. Enjoy now or cellar for a few years.

The wine is normally deep yellow to light gold coloured. Melon and peach fruit flavours are well integrated with light buttery, cashew nut, barrel ferment characters. An intensely flavoured, elegant wine with great balance of fruit, oak and acid, a wine to cellar for five years or more to enhance its richness and complexity.

Quality, reliable and affordable.

A crafted quality product, select grapes and skilful winemaking.

Premium quality, the pursuit of excellence.

The making of
Eileen Hardy Chardonnay

The vineyard.

The fermentation, first in stainless steel and then in oak barrels.

Further storage in oak barrels.

The wine is sampled and tasted regularly to follow its development.

After selection and blending, the wine is bottled and packaged.

*C*hardonnay vines are grown in all the wine regions of Australia and many styles of wine are produced. Some producers make a range of styles and may source grapes from a number of viticultural areas.

A Selection Of The Diverse Tastes Of Australian Chardonnay

Northern Territory

Queensland

Western Australia

South Australia

New South Wales

Victoria

Tasmania

Western Australia

Perth
Evans and Tate
Sandalford
Houghton
Olive Farm

Australind
Capel Vale
Killerby

Margaret River
Leeuwin
Cape Mantelle
Cullens
Vasse Felix
Pierro
Chateau Xanadu

Great Southern
Goundrey
Plantagenet

New South Wales

Port Macquarie
Cassegrain

Mudgee
Craigmoor
Montrose
Thistle Hill
Miramar
Botobolar

Riverina
McWilliams
Miranda
De Bortoli

Cowra
Cowra Wines
Richmond Grove

Hunter Valley
Lake's Folly
Rothbury
Arrowfield
Tyrrells
Rosemount
Reynolds
Sutherland
McGuigan Brothers
Pepper Tree
Serenella
Wyndham Estate

Queensland

Granite Belt
Robinsons
Ballandean

Ipswich
Ironbark Ridge

Tasmania

North East
Pipers Brook
Heemskerk

Central Coast
Freycinet

South East
Moorilla
Hood
Fishburn and O'Keefe

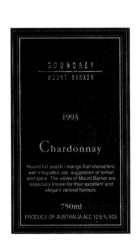

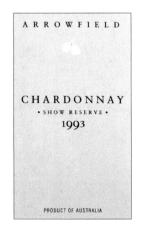

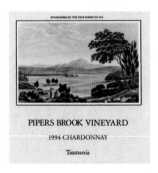

Victoria

Yarra Valley
Coldstream Hills
De Bortoli
Fergusson
Tarrawarra
St Hubert's
Shantell
Yarra Burn

Mornington Peninsula
Stoniers
Dromana
T'Gallant
Moorooduc
Hickinbotham
Tuerong Estate
De Bortoli
Main Ridge

Geelong
Bannockburn
Idyll
Scotchmans Hill

Central Victoria
Tisdall

Goulburn Valley
Mitchelton
Chateau Tahbilk

Murray River / Sunraysia
Trentham Estate
Sunnycliff

North-East Victoria
Brown Brothers
HJT Vineyards
St Leonards
Giaconda
Campbells

Pyrenees
Chateau Remy
Summerfield
Dalwhinnie
Mount Avoca

South Australia

Clare
Grossett
Taylors

Coonawarra / Padthaway
Wynns
Hollick
Katnook
Bowen Estate
Leconfield
Lindemans
Orlando
Brand's
Mildara

Barossa Valley
St Hallett
Krondorf
Orlando
Miranda Rovalley Estate
Grant Burge
Saltram
Chateau Yaldara
Wolf Blass Wines
Richmond Grove

Eden Valley
Mountadam
Grand Cru
Henschke
Craneford

Adelaide Hills
Petaluma
Shaw and Smith
Stafford Ridge

Reynella / McLaren Vale
Chapel Hill
Wirra Wirra
Hardys
Woodstock
Richard Hamilton
Hazelgrove
Andrew Garrett
Pirramimma

Adelaide
Tolley

Riverland
Angoves
Kingston Estate

Chardonnay is an ideal seafood wine. It is also a good accompaniment to pasta, chicken and veal. Richly flavoured, layered and complex Chardonnays are suited to a range of full flavoured dishes.

Wood ducks in flight over Mountadam vineyard, Eden Valley.

1993 *Coldstream Hills*

R E S E R V E
C H A R D O N N A Y

Reserve

750 ML LI ALC. 14.0% VOL

BOTTLED BY COLDSTREAM WINEMAKERS LIMITED
LOT 6 MADDENS LANE, COLDSTREAM VICTORIA
VICTORIA PRODUCE OF AUSTRALIA

PETALUMA

1992 CHARDONNAY

750ml

PRODUCE OF AUSTRALIA BOTTLED AT PICCADILLY, SA

LEEUWIN ESTATE   John Coburn

1990
Margaret River
Chardonnay

PRODUCE OF WESTERN AUSTRALIA
ALCOHOL 13.9% BY VOLUME

*S*ome of
Australia's
renowned
Chardonnay wines.

MOUNTADAM

CHARDONNAY 1992

13.5% ALC/VOL   AUSTRALIAN WINE 750 ml

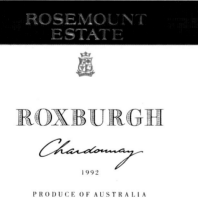

ROSEMOUNT
ESTATE

ROXBURGH

Chardonnay

1992

PRODUCE OF AUSTRALIA

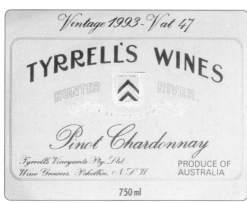

Vintage 1993 - Vat 47

TYRRELL'S WINES

HUNTER   RIVER

Pinot Chardonnay

Tyrrell's Vineyards Pty Ltd
Wine Growers, Pokolbin, N.S.W.   PRODUCE OF
AUSTRALIA

750 ml

Type and intensity
of varietal character
depends on:

Where the grapes
were grown

How ripe the grapes
were at harvest

How the vines
were managed

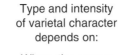

Examples of varietal character descriptors

The combination of descriptors will vary from wine to wine.

*A*ssessing dry white table wines

Wines may be coloured various shades of straw and yellow.

Young wines may have green tinges.

Older wines develop deep yellow/golden colours.

The wine should be clear. In some wines crystals of tartrate may be present. A small amount of these crystals is acceptable. They are not harmful.

Wines may exhibit primary and/or developed fruit characters and in some wines other characters derived from wine-making.

Look for
• intensity and balance of characters
• complexity

Look for
• intensity and balance of characters
• balance of acid/sweetness
• freshness
• complexity
• pleasant mouthfeel
• length and persistency of flavour

Riesling:	*Primary fruit characters* floral, fragrant, perfumed, rose-petal, cold tea, pear, lemon, citrus, lime, grapefruit, pineapple, fruity, passionfruit, tropical fruit. *Developed fruit characters* toasty, honey, kerosene.
Gewürztraminer:	*Primary fruit characters* floral, spicy, perfumed, rose, lime, lychee, lavender.
Frontignac:	*Primary fruit characters* floral, perfumed, scented, aromatic, spicy, rose, blossom.
Sauvignon Blanc:	*Primary fruit characters* vegetal, asparagus, capsicum, tomato bush, herbaceous, freshly cut grass, grassy, gooseberry, passionfruit, melon, tropical fruit.
Semillon:	*Primary fruit characters* herbaceous, pea pod, green, grassy, flinty, straw, gooseberry, apple, quince, lemon, lime, citrus, fig, tropical fruit. *Developed fruit characters* toasty, honey, fig, nutty.
Colombard:	*Primary fruit characters* herbaceous, grassy, apple, citrus, lime, melon, passionfruit, tropical fruit, honeysuckle.
Chenin Blanc:	*Primary fruit characters* herbaceous, herbal, grassy, floral, sweaty, honey.
Verdelho:	*Primary fruit characters* herbaceous, spicy, grassy, melon, pineapple, guava, honeysuckle, tropical fruit, fruit salad.
Viognier:	*Primary fruit characters* lemon, citrus, mint.
Marsanne:	*Primary fruit characters* lemon, peach, honey. *Developed fruit characters* honeysuckle.
Chardonnay:	*Primary fruit characters* cucumber, tobacco, apple, grapefruit, lemon, lime, pineapple, melon, gooseberry, rockmelon, fig, peach, tropical fruit, fruit salad. *Developed fruit characters* toasty, honey, fig, nutty, cashew.

THE WINEMAKING PROCESS

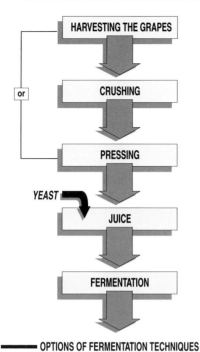

HARVESTING THE GRAPES

↓

or

CRUSHING

↓

PRESSING

↓

YEAST →

JUICE

↓

FERMENTATION

↓

━━━ OPTIONS OF FERMENTATION TECHNIQUES ━━━

| IN STAINLESS STEEL TANKS | IN OAK BARRELS | PARTIALLY IN STAINLESS STEEL THEN TRANSFERRED TO OAK BARRELS | TYPE OF YEAST | VARIOUS DEGREES OF JUICE CLARIFICATION |

with or without malo-lactic fermentation
and/or
with or without yeast lees contact with the wine
after fermentation is complete

CLARIFICATION AND STABILISATION

↓

The actual characters present in any wine depend on the characters that were present in the grapes, how the wine was made and the age of the wine.

STORAGE

↓

STAINLESS STEEL TANKS   OAK BARRELS

PREPARATION FOR BOTTLING

BOTTLING

↓

MATURATION IN THE BOTTLE

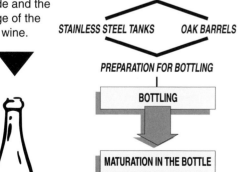

*O*ptimum temperature range for enjoying white wine:
10-12°C; the higher end of the range is more appropriate for full-bodied styles.

Wines made from the varieties Sauvignon Blanc, Semillon, Verdelho, Marsanne, Viognier and Chardonnay may have additional characters that come from malo-lactic fermentation, barrel fermentation, time on lees and barrel storage.

Malo-lactic fermentation (MLF)
creamy, buttery, butterscotch, yogurt, caramel.

The lactic acid formed has a less acid taste than the malic acid, and the conversion thus results in a better acid balance in the wine; the wine tastes softer on the palate.

Barrel fermentation/time on lees
creamy, yeasty, vegemite, bonox, marmite, cheesy, bread, toasty, leesy.

Wines that have had time on lees generally have improved mouth-feel, often described by saying that the wines have a creamy or cheesy texture on the palate.

Barrel fermentation/barrel storage
vanilla, toasty, sawdust, cedar, olives, spicy, bacon, coconut, pencil shavings, dusty, cashews, smoky, burnt, caramel, raisin, charred.

The alcohol level of these wines is usually between 11 and 14% alcohol by volume.

𝒲ine - a choice of styles for every palate

Many producers make a range of wines that offer a choice of styles and price points. The wines may be different because they have been made from different vineyards or by different winemaking techniques reflecting different philosophies. In this section, we discuss wines that offer further choice in enjoying the taste of wine.

Organic wine

During the last decade there has been increasing interest in and demand for organically grown food products. Some producers are now offering this choice to wine drinkers. Gil Wahlquist pioneered organic grape growing in Australia at his Botobolar Vineyard near Mudgee.

Botobolar Vineyard makes a range of organic wines, including a Chardonnay, a Shiraz and a Marsanne.

Adam Wynn of Mountadam Vineyard was instrumental in forming the Organic Vignerons Association of Australia, and now there are a number of producers who offer the choice of organic wines. There has been a focus on the export market, but in the future you can expect to see more organic wines on the Australian market as well.

Mountadam's organically produced Shiraz wine.

The aim of organic producers is to create and work with a balance between the vines and nature.

The procedures for growing grapes organically prohibit the use of most synthetic pesticides and manufactured fertilisers. Copper and sulphur based pesticides, bacterial insecticides and fertilisers from natural sources are permitted. The use of sprays in the vineyard to control disease is minimal, but this approach is also followed in all Australian vineyards (either organic or non-organic). We are lucky that many vinegrowing areas of Australia have warm, sunny and dry climates during the growing season, conditions which require minimal use of sprays and which favour a clean, green image for Australian vineyards.

Penfolds' organic vineyard at Clare.

Organic wine is made from grapes which are not only grown organically, but are also processed in accordance with the standards of organic winemaking practice. These include the use of micro-organisms (yeast and bacteria) and certain chemicals, such as sulphur dioxide, carbon dioxide, natural acids and some fining agents.

Organic wine is different in that the practices required in the vineyard and the range of additives and fining agents that can be used are limited. The allowed level of sulphur dioxide is also lower than in other wines.

For those people who believe in and support the philosophy of organic agriculture and food, these wines provide a guarantee that they were made in this way. Organic wines carry a certification number on the label to indicate that the grapes came from a certified organic vineyard and that the wine was made according to organic winemaking standards.

The use of additives and fining agents in wine

The following comments relate to all wines, including organic wines.

The use of small amounts of additives and of fining agents is generally necessary to ensure that the wine will be clear, stable and sound, have longevity and be enjoyable to taste.

The use of sulphur dioxide and carbon dioxide throughout the winemaking process aids in preventing oxidation, which may otherwise cause undesirable tastes in the wine. The addition of sulphur dioxide to the grapes and juice also assures that the fermentation is conducted by the desirable yeast.

Although micro-organisms (both those naturally present on the grapes and those added during winemaking) can be removed during the winemaking process through settling and filtration, there is a very small chance that some may remain in the finished product. The addition of sulphur dioxide in small amounts to both organic and other wines at bottling lessens the chance of oxidation and any microbrial growth; there is less chance of the wine being spoilt.

The use of some fining agents is necessary to ensure that the wine remains clear. Grapes contain compounds such as proteins which, when carried over into the wine, may precipitate from solution and cause a haze. The use of fining agents such as bentonite, a natural clay product, to remove the proteins from the wine prevents haze formation. Fining agents are also used to improve sensory aspects of the wine, for example, egg whites can be used to fine a red wine to soften the tannin sensation.

Organic wines, apart from differences in levels and types of additives and fining agents, are made in very much the same way as other wines. Chardonnay, for example, can be made according to organic standards and still be barrel fermented and stored on lees, undergo malo-lactic fermentation and be stored in wood. The barrels, though, must be specially marked and used only for organic wines.

The organic approach to making wine can produce wines that range from average to premium quality products. Organic wine, like any other wine, relies very much on the quality of the grapes and the skills of the winemaker.

Preservative free wine

Some people are very sensitive to sulphur dioxide and even the small additions that are made in making wines can cause concern to these people. Some companies such as Hardys and Botobolar Vineyard make a white and a red wine that have no sulphur dioxide added during the winemaking process. These wines are labelled *preservative free*.

These wines are recommended for people with a low tolerance to sulphur dioxide or those seeking to avoid preservatives in their diet.

Experience with the ageing potential of these wines is limited and generally it is recommended that they be consumed soon after bottling.

Reduced alcohol wines

A number of producers make wines that have lower alcohol levels.

Seppelt's reduced alcohol wines are made by an innovative technique (Method Encore™) that allows the aromas and flavours of a wine to be separated from the rest of the wine, which is then carefully vacuum distilled to remove the alcohol. The aroma and flavour fraction is then returned to the de-alcoholised portion. This is blended with an equal proportion of full-strength wine to give a wine of about 6% alcohol v/v, but still with its full quota of distinctive aromas and flavours.

Reduced alcohol wines from other producers are made by similar methods.

These reduced alcohol wines offer further choice to wine consumers as they select wine for different occasions.

ENJOY WINE IN MODERATION

Enjoying wine is all about choosing and tasting different wines. The occasion, as well as price, health and lifestyle considerations, may influence that choice at any particular time. Whether the wine be organic or otherwise, preservative added or free, full-strength or reduced strength, it is important to enjoy wine in moderation.

Botrytis cinerea growing on a bunch of grapes in the vineyard.

The golden brown juice oozing from the press.

De Bortoli's famous Botrytis-affected Semillon wine, the 'Noble One'.

The finished product.

Semi-sweet and sweet white wine

Semi-sweet and sweet white wines, like other wines, are made in a range of styles. Many wine drinkers were introduced to wine through these styles. The sweet, fruity tastes of semi-sweet white wines provided an easy transition into the world of wine, which for many has led to the discovery of all the diversity and interest that wine has to offer.

Australia's sweeter wine styles are made predominantly from the varieties Riesling and Semillon. Their complex array of rich aromas and flavours, mixed with luscious sweet tastes, yet balanced with refreshing acidity, have enticed many a wine lover to explore the range of products offered by these styles.

Some are wines made from grapes affected by a mould, *Botrytis cinerea*; the murky, golden brown juice extracted from these apparently 'rotten' grapes produces a golden coloured, very sweet wine with extraordinarily rich and complex tastes.

Australia is lucky to have many areas suitable for the production of these botrytised styles. Superb botrytised Rieslings are produced from areas such as Padthaway, Coonawarra and the Barossa Ranges of South Australia, while the Riverina region of New South Wales is renowned for its botrytised Semillons. These wines, with their complexity and lusciousness, complement a range of full-flavoured foods, cheeses and rich desserts; they are wines to be savoured throughout the meal, but especially towards the end of the meal.

Sweet white table wine (botrytis-affected)

Who would have thought that a mould could possibly play a role in producing such wonderfully complex wines? But *Botrytis cinerea*, known also as *Noble Rot,* does just that. *Botrytis cinerea* is one of the many moulds which occur wherever fruit and vegetables are grown. Whereas most mould infections are undesirable, producers of these rich, luscious, white wines wait anxiously to see the signs of *Botrytis cinerea* on their grapes. When *Botrytis cinerea* grows on grapes it can transform firm, ripe, flavoursome berries into shrivelled, constricted packages of very sweet, intensely flavoured and complex tastes.

Natural infection

At the later stages of ripening and when temperature conditions are just right, and usually when the humidity is between 85 and 95%, the botrytis spores germinate and send their 'roots' (hyphae) through the grape skin and into the outermost cells of the flesh. They form a tangled mass just below the skin of the berry and as the mould grows they extract water from the berry. The berry shrivels and the sugar and flavours become more concentrated.

But botrytis infection also causes other changes in the berry. It induces new aromas and flavours in the juice of the berry, and wine made from these berries has distinctive *apricot, marmalade, caramel* and *honey* characters. As the mould grows the skin takes on a purplish colour and the juice becomes more yellow. Some of the acids of the berries are also broken down. Additionally, glycerol can be excreted into the juice of the berry. The overall effect is that the juice becomes very viscous.

The berry may lose up to 50% of its original weight and one berry may produce only a few drops of golden juice with a sugar content of 20° Baumé or greater. The greater the level of infection, the greater the degree of shrivelling and the higher the concentration of sugars, aromas and flavour compounds. It is important that the berry remains intact during the growth of the botrytis, since if the berry splits other undesirable moulds and infections can grow. Juice from split berries can be infected with wild yeast (present on the grape skin), and the juice can become volatile.

In some vineyards the right conditions will occur every year, whereas in others they may only occur every few years. It is only in favourable years that this style of wine can be produced naturally.

Artificial infection

In regions where natural botrytis infection does not occur, some winemakers make this style of wine by artificially inducing botrytis. Primo Estate is a small winery in the Adelaide Plains region of South Australia, an area where botrytis infection seldom occurs, yet Joe Grilli, the winemaker, consistently produces a rich botrytis-affected Riesling wine. Here the grapes are carefully picked and any grapes showing the slightest sign of splitting are rejected. The grapes are laid out in trays in a room where high humidity is induced. They are then sprayed with a solution containing botrytis spores that have been specially bred in the laboratory. The high humidity simulates the desired conditions and encourages the botrytis spores to grow and infect the grapes, causing them to shrivel. At the desired degree of infection, the grapes are crushed and/or pressed and the winemaking commences.

How these wines are made

Once the desired stage of shrivel and sugar concentration is reached the grapes are hand harvested. Bunches may be left on the vine until the desired degree of infection is obtained.

The grapes are then crushed and pressed. *Botrytis cinerea* produces an enzyme called *laccase*, which can cause oxidation of the juice, and higher than usual additions of sulphur dioxide to the juice may be necessary to inhibit the laccase activity. Sometimes the whole bunches are pressed directly.

The viscous liquid that oozes from the press is clarified by settling and/or filtration. The juice, when free of solids, is pumped to a fermentation vessel and yeast added to initiate the fermentation.

The process requires specially selected yeast that can tolerate and ferment these high-sugar juices. Even then the fermentation will be very slow, sometimes taking several weeks or months to reach the correct balance of alcohol and sugar level required in the final wine.

In the production of these styles of wine the yeast can produce high levels of volatile acidity, as well as fermenting the sugar. It is difficult to make these styles without this influence, which if not-overpowering should not be regarded as a fault. In fact, certain levels can add complexity to the nose and palate.

Once the fermentation has reached the desired stage it is stopped and the wine is clarified and cold stabilised. Botrytis affected grapes contain large polymeric compounds (called glucans) which can block filter pads, and so clarification of the wine can be difficult. Clarification is normally achieved by allowing the wine to settle over a long period of time. Some producers use equipment such as centrifuges and various filtration systems to clarify the wine.

Wines made from Riesling grapes are stored in stainless steel tanks, while those made from Semillon grapes may be stored in oak barrels prior to being bottled. These wines are often matured in the bottle before being released.

The production of these botrytis style wines is very costly. Not only does the winemaker lose about half the weight of the grapes as they shrivel on the vine or on the trays, but making these wines is also risky and very labour intensive. They are usually sold in half bottles.

Australia produces two main styles of these botrytis-affected wines, one made from Riesling grapes and the other from Semillon grapes.

Botrytis-affected Riesling

What you will see on the label

These wines may be labelled Botrytis Riesling, Botrytis-affected, Noble Riesling, or Noble Rot Riesling. You may also see the German terms 'Beerenauslese' and 'Trockenbeerenauslese'. These terms indicate that the wine is very sweet, rich and complex. 'Trockenbeerenauslese' is the sweetest and most complex style.

Botrytis-affected Semillon

What you will see on the label

These wines will be labelled Botrytis Semillon, Noble Semillon, Botrytis-affected Semillon or Sauternes. However, the term Sauternes will eventually disappear from Australian labels. Even though this name change may not occur for some time, a number of producers have already deleted the word Sauternes from their labels.

SENSORY FEATURES OF BOTRYTIS-AFFECTED RIESLING AND SEMILLON WINES

APPEARANCE

The colour of these wines ranges from yellow to deep golden. After being swirled in the glass, these wines, being quite viscous, may adhere to the sides of the glass forming syrupy tears.

AROMAS AND FLAVOURS

These wines have a mixture of primary fruit, developed fruit, and botrytis induced aromas and flavours. The mixing of the different sensations produces a complex array which may vary depending on the ripeness of the grapes and the degree of botrytis infection when the grapes are harvested, and the age of the wine.

The apricot, marmalade-like characters are typical of the flavours that come from botrytis affected grapes.

In some wines volatility may be obvious, but should not be regarded as a fault if it is not overpowering. It can add lift and complexity to the powerful fruit and botrytis derived flavours of these wines.

Riesling

Some descriptors for this mix of aromas, bouquet and flavours include: *citrus, lime, pineapple, quince, crab-apple jelly, floral, perfume, passionfruit, mango, tropical fruit, fruit salad, cumquat, apricot, dried apricot, honey, toffee, caramel, golden syrup* and *treacle*. Various combinations will be present in different wines.

Semillon

A mix of smells and tastes including some of the following: *herbs, spice, cloves, orange peel, mandarin peel, marmalade, apricot, dried apricot, honey, toffee, butterscotch, nutty, almond* and *marzipan*. Various combinations will be present in different wines.

THE PALATE

The palate of these wines, like the nose, should be rich and complex. A feature is the textural effect on the palate, often described by terms such as *viscous, luscious, rich, oily* and *unctuous*.

Although these wines are luscious and sweet they should finish dry, the sweetness being balanced by drying acidity and/or the contribution of phenolics from oak storage as is the case with Semillon.

Botrytis-affected Semillon

De Bortoli Wines has led the way in establishing the Riverina as a prestige area for the production of Botrytis Semillon. Many wineries in this region now produce this wine style. Towards the end of the vintage period frequent rain and fog help create humid conditions, which favour the growth of botrytis on the grapes. Normally, rain at this time would be detrimental, since the vines would take up water, causing the berries to split. However, because the soils here are free-draining the water drains away readily. The combination of the soil and the climate ensures that botrytis develops and grows regularly in these Riverina vineyards.

Botrytis Semillon wines are also made in other Australian wine regions if conditions are favourable for the growth of botrytis in that year.

Although the wineries of the Riverina region are known for their Botrytis Semillons, many wineries and particularly the larger producers, have vineyards in or obtain fruit from other regions, and thus they produce a diversity of wine styles under their labels.

Miranda obtains fruit from the King, Eden, Clare and Barossa Valleys and the McLaren Vale and Coonawarra regions for their range of white and red table wines. You can sample these either at the Miranda winery in Griffith or at their Rovalley Estates winery in the Barossa Valley.

De Bortoli's winery and restaurant complex in the Yarra Valley offers a great opportunity to enjoy fine food and to taste their range of cooler climate wines from Pinot Noir, Chardonnay, Cabernet Sauvignon and Shiraz.

Try these botrytis-affected Riesling and Semillon wines with strongly, flavoured cheeses, rich liver pates, dried fruit and nuts, and rich desserts.

A tasting experience

Some wines to try:

Botrytis-affected Semillon	Botrytis-affected Riesling
De Bortoli	Primo Estate
Miranda	Hardys
Wilton Estate	Yalumba
Rossetto	Mitchelton
Peter Lehmann	Tollana
Morris	Henschke
	d'Arenberg
	St Huberts

Wyangan Estate's 'Golden Botrytis': a premium botrytis-affected semillon from Miranda Wines in the Riverina region.

103

Semi-sweet and sweet white wine (non-botrytis-affected)

Generally, the semi-sweet styles contain between about 10 and 30 grams of sugar per litre, while the sweeter styles can have from around 30 to 100 or more grams per litre. These sugar levels are referred to as *residual sugar*. The primary objective of the winemaker is to balance the sweet taste with crisp acidity so that the combination of flavours, sweetness and freshness provides a pleasing, enjoyable tasting experience. These wines are made from an assortment of grape varieties including Riesling, Gewürztraminer, Frontignac, Muscat Gordo Blanco and Semillon.

How these wines are made

1 Semi-sweet and sweet styles of white wine can be made by allowing the juice to ferment to dryness and then adding concentrated grape juice to sweeten the wine to the desired sugar level.

Traditionally, the sweet wines from the Hunter Valley are made this way. For example, Lindemans Hunter River Porphyry is made from Semillon grapes grown in their Hunter Valley vineyards. The juice is fermented to dryness and then a concentrated and very sweet grape juice is added to increase the sugar level to about 100 grams or more per litre. Although these sweet wines can be enjoyed as fresh young wines, they are at their best when allowed to mature in the bottle for a number of years. In time these wines develop lovely *apricot, toffee, honey, caramel* and *marmalade-like* characters to complement their luscious, lingering tastes. Lindemans also produces a Reserve Porphyry, of similar style, from carefully selected premium quality grapes from other prime grape growing regions.

2 Another way to produce these styles of white wine is to stop the fermentation before all the grape sugars are converted to alcohol. This leaves unfermented sugar (residual sugar) present in the wine.

For example, if the grapes are harvested at about 12º Baumé, and the fermentation is stopped after 11 of these units have been converted to alcohol, the wine will contain about 11% v/v alcohol and about 20 grams per litre of sugar. However, if the grapes are harvested at about 15º Baumé

and the fermentation is stopped after 11 of these units have been converted to alcohol, the wine will contain about 11% alcohol and about 70 grams per litre of sugar. For these sweeter styles, the grapes need to attain higher sugar levels in the vineyard. Not only will the sugar level be higher, but there will usually also be a greater intensity of flavours in the grapes and the wines should be more flavoursome and luscious.

Semi-sweet and sweet white wines are made in a similar manner to dry white wines except that the fermentation may be stopped part way through. Some winemakers hold the juice in contact with the skins for a short period prior to pressing to increase colour and flavour. The juice is fermented with specially selected yeasts to the stage when the winemaker considers the balance of alcohol and sugar is appropriate for the particular style of wine. The fermentation can be stopped by chilling the wine (which reduces yeast activity and also helps to retain fresh fruit characters), by the addition of sulphur dioxide (which prevents microbiological activity) and by filtration (to remove the yeast). After fermentation ceases the wine is clarified, stabilised and bottled.

Semi-sweet styles are normally made to be enjoyed as young wines, while the sweeter styles may benefit from maturation.

The suitability of any batch of grapes for a particular style relies very much on the sugar content and flavour profile of the grapes at harvest.

<u>Natural ripening</u>

To achieve these higher sugar levels, the grapes are left on the vine way past the normal harvest period, sometimes up to 4 weeks. ºBaumé levels of up to about 15 may be achieved naturally, but this depends on the climatic conditions prevalent during the later stages of ripening. In addition, at these later stages of ripening, the berries can lose water, resulting in berry shrivel. As this happens the sugars and flavours of the berries are concentrated, making the grapes more suitable for the sweeter styles. Wines made from these grapes may be labelled *late picked* or *late harvested*.

*C*ane-cut

To reach the higher grape sugar levels required for the sweet to very sweet styles, techniques other than natural ripening and berry shrivel are normally required. A technique sometimes used at the later stages of ripening to induce berry shrivel is to cut the canes of the vine and allow them to hang on the trellis wire. The sugar and flavours, present in the berries when the cane is cut, are concentrated as the berries shrivel. This encourages berry shrivel to occur at a stage when desirable flavours are present and often avoids the development of overripe characters. The wines are labelled *cane-cut* or as in the case of Mount Horrocks, *cordon-cut*.

What you will see on the label

Words that you may see on the label are *late picked, late harvested* and the generic terms *moselle, spätlese* and *auslese*.

These generic terms have been borrowed, and are used to describe the various categories of the sweet white wines of Germany, but they do not necessarily reflect similar wine styles here. In Australia, these terms are used rather broadly to indicate the level of sweetness/style of the wine: moselle is normally used for slightly sweet wines, spätlese for medium sweet wines and auslese for sweeter styles. However, these should only be used as a guide, since in Australia different producers' classifications for any category can vary considerably from one another. In time, Australian wines will no longer be labelled as Moselle, since this term relates to a wine from the area along the Mosel River in Germany.

You will find some of the sweeter wine styles labelled as Lindemans Porphyry or as Sauternes from Lindemans or McWilliam's.

SENSORY FEATURES OF SEMI-SWEET AND SWEET STYLES (NON-BOTRYTIS AFFECTED)

APPEARANCE

These wines range in colour from light yellow through to gold. Deeper yellow, golden colours are associated with the sweeter styles, particularly when they have aged.

AROMAS AND FLAVOURS

The sensory characters associated with any wine depend on the variety/varieties from which it is made. Typically semi-sweet and sweet wines are intensely *floral, fragrant* and *fruity*, while the sweeter styles may be more complex, with *honeyed, marmalade-like* characters.

THE PALATE

These wines vary from light-bodied through to full-bodied styles.

The light-bodied styles contain lower sugar levels and generally have a fragrant, flavoursome palate. The finish should be clean and fresh.

The medium- to full-bodied styles contain higher sugar levels and may have more intense and complex aroma and flavour profiles. The palate of the sweeter styles should be rich and luscious, have palate weight, good mouth-feel and a long finish. Even though these wines are sweet to very sweet they should not be cloying, but rather should finish with a drying sensation in the mouth due to balanced acid.

A tasting experience

The wines below provide an introduction to the taste of semi-sweet and sweet white wine. They differ in the varieties from which they were made and in their level of sweetness, progressing generally from low to high levels.

Mildara's vineyards in Coonawarra.

Dry red table wine

Tasting red wines introduces an additional array of sensory descriptors to the language of wine. It is also in red wines that the taste and feel of 'the tannins' is encountered. New dimensions are added to the adventure and pleasure of tasting wine.

These are wines made from black grapes, where the mixture of juice, skins and seeds is kept together after crushing and during fermentation, until the winemaker decides that sufficient colour, tannin and flavour have been extracted from the skins. Most are stored for some time in oak barrels and most undergo a malo-lactic fermentation. Some are ready to drink when young, while others can be enjoyed over many years.

Australian red wine styles range from rosé and light-bodied reds through to full-bodied red wines. They are made from a single variety or a blend of different varieties, and with many different winemaking philosophies. Thus, in Australian red wines you can expect to discover both an abundance of flavour and many different flavours.

Light- to medium-bodied styles are normally made from the varieties Grenache and Pinot Noir. Light-bodied reds may also be produced from Shiraz, Cabernet Sauvignon and other varieties if extraction from skins is limited during fermentation. Generally, these wines are low in tannin, do not exhibit strong oak characters and are refreshing, drink-early styles.

Medium- to full-bodied styles are normally made from the varieties Cabernet Sauvignon, Shiraz, Cabernet Franc, Merlot, Malbec, Durif and sometimes from Pinot Noir and Grenache. These wines may show complexity due to the influences of oak storage, malo-lactic fermentation and age. They are more tannic and may be astringent when young. Most have potential to improve with age. They are often made as blends such as Cabernet Sauvignon/Shiraz, a classic Australian red wine blend which combines the elegance of Cabernet Sauvignon with the richness of Shiraz.

At the far end of the red wine spectrum are full-bodied, complex, richly flavoured Shiraz wines.

$\mathcal{R}$ed wines: how they change with time

Tannins

Black grapes contain compounds that can form tannins in wine. Anthocyanins (the coloured compounds in the skin) and other phenolics of the grape, once extracted during winemaking, can combine with each other to form tannins. These tannins interact with the saliva in the mouth, nullifying its lubricating action, and thus the mouth feels dry. Wines that have this feeling in the mouth are described as astringent. The tannins are initially small and then gradually combine to form larger tannins. The more dissolved oxygen present in the wine, the faster this maturation process occurs.

The interaction between tannins and saliva is stronger when the tannins are smaller. This is why some young wines which are high in tannins may be very astringent. The larger tannins which form as the wine ages do not react to the same extent with the saliva; the impact of the tannins in the mouth is less astringent and the wine is more pleasing to taste. Now the feel of the tannins is more textural, often described as grainy. There is now greater opportunity for the flavours of the wine, and particularly the more subtle flavours that come with age, to manifest themselves in the taste of the wine. Thus many wines made from Cabernet Sauvignon and Shiraz, or blends of these and other varieties, require time to mature and soften so that both their flavours and mouthfeel can be fully appreciated.

Colour

The anthocyanins and the smaller tannins are red coloured, whereas the large tannins are brown. Thus, the colour of red wines can change with time from red, red/purple and sometimes almost black (in young wines with high concentrations of anthocyanins) to brick red, red brown and brown. How quickly the progression occurs depends on the initial intensity of colour and how the wine is managed in the cellar and during storage.

Aroma and flavour

Alongside the modification of the tannin structure with time, aroma and flavour characters also change. Developed characters become predominant. Maturation and ageing, properly conducted, increase the complexity and quality of the wine.

Other reactions also take place. Some of the acids and alcohol present can react to form volatile compounds called esters and aldehydes, but the impact of these changes on the bouquet of the wine is generally regarded as minimal.

Overall changes

During storage in the winery, in either oak barrels or tanks, the aromas, flavours, colours and tannins of the wine are modified as the wine matures. These processes continue, albeit more slowly, even after the wine is bottled.

Winemaking techniques that give greater extraction of tannins, and where some oxygen pick-up occurs during storage, are more suited to grapes with high levels of flavour, colour and tannins. Although it may take some time for the tannins to soften (in some cases many years), it is likely that there will still be plenty of primary and developed fruit characters present to give enjoyable drinking.

If fruit intensity is low, the requirements change. Winemaking techniques that result in a high level of extraction of compounds from the skin and seeds may produce a wine with plenty of tannins but, by the time those tannins soften, the fruit characters will have matured way past their optimum. Cooler ferments, less time on skins and careful, controlled extraction techniques are more suitable for this type of fruit.

The skill of the winemaker is to balance the extraction of colour and tannins with the intensity of fruit characters present in any batch of grapes. This comes from experience and is part of the art of winemaking.

An example of how red wine colour can change with time.

When is the best stage to enjoy red wines?

The stage when the taste of any wine is at its pinnacle is difficult to define. It depends on individual preference and whether you enjoy the vibrant aromas and flavours and the assertive astringency of youth, or the more subtle bouquet, flavours and textures that come with time. Many wines are enjoyed most when the flavours and textures of youth fuse with those of age to give a complex but harmonious taste. These are wines which have rich, enticing flavours, finely grained tannins and a pleasing mouthfeel.

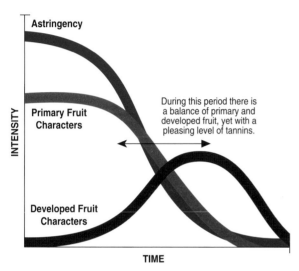

A representation of how the sensations of primary and developed fruit characters and astringency may change with time. Each wine will have different levels of intensity of these characters and a different pattern of change.

How long will a wine improve in the bottle?

There is no definitive answer to this question. Many winemakers are now making wines that are full of flavour and have moderate levels of tannins. These wines are soft in the mouth even as young wines; they are wines that can often be enjoyed a few years after they are made and can also age well for five to ten years.

However, wines that have the propensity to age gracefully over many years (ten, twenty years or more) will have, as a rule, intense flavours coupled with high levels of supple tannins and fresh acidity; they are wines that are perfectly balanced and structured. They can be medium-bodied or full-bodied wines. Generally they come from well-managed vines grown in cool to warm and warm sites. Often the yields are low.

Storage conditions

Wines will age for varying lengths of time, depending on their initial intensity of fruit characters, how they are made and how they are stored. Not everyone will have a place that provides ideal cellaring conditions. However, as a guide, bottles of wine should be stored on their sides in a place

- where the temperature is about 13ºC, and more importantly where there is minimal fluctuation of temperature;
- where it is not too dry or too moist, where the relative humidity is ideally about 90%; and
- which is dark, away from vibrations and free of odours.

Sometimes, if the cork does not fit the bottle exactly or if there has been movement of the cork in the bottle during storage (mainly due to excessive temperature fluctuations), wine may start to leak between the cork and the side of the bottle. If this seepage continues, the wine should be consumed, or professionally recorked to reduce further wine loss, cork shrinkage and possible oxidation.

The most important issue is to attempt to avoid storage conditions that are prone to temperature fluctuations in the first place.

Lighter bodied red wines
Rosé

In Australia this style of wine is made from a number of grape varieties, but most often from Grenache or Cabernet Sauvignon.

Rosé style wines are made by one of two basic methods.

- In the first method, the grapes are picked at lower sugar levels (about 10-11° Baumé) with higher amounts of acid, and have cherry, raspberry and fruity type flavours, features necessary for the production of crisp, fruity, light-bodied wines. After crushing, fermentation is conducted at cool temperatures and skin contact is minimal, just one or two days depending on the desired level of flavour, colour and tannin extraction. After transferring the wine to the press, the free run juice is fermented just as if it were a white wine. There is no malolactic fermentation or oak contact. The finished wine is normally a bright crimson colour with a light, soft, fruity palate and a crisp acid finish. It is ideal for drinking when young and soon after bottling.

- Another method is to drain off part of the fermenting juice at an early stage of a normal red wine fermentation. The run off juice with low colour is fermented and processed similarly to a white wine to produce a rosé style. The remaining liquid (still in contact with the skins) is fermented to produce a more highly coloured and flavoured dry red wine, due to a higher skin to juice ratio.

Houghton's Rosé is made from Cabernet Sauvignon grapes sourced from a number of Western Australian vineyards. It consistently shows all the characters of an excellent rosé style: vivid crimson colour, attractive berry-like aromas and flavours and a soft, flavoursome palate with fresh acidity on the finish.

The Cab Mac Process

It was Louis Pasteur who in 1872 first observed that something happens inside the berry when grapes are placed into a sealed container without any oxygen. But it was not until 1934 that another Frenchman, Professor Michael Flanzy, discovered what was occurring inside the berry. Under these conditions an enzymatic fermentation occurs inside the cells of the intact berry and malic acid is converted to alcohol.

Other changes also take place inside the berry. Aromas and flavours including those similar to cherries and cinnamon are produced. The overall process is referred to as *carbonic maceration.*

Flanzy developed a winemaking procedure which has become known as the Carbonic Maceration Process. It is used in the Beaujolais region of France to produce light-bodied, fruity styles of red wine from the grape variety Gamay. Bunches of grapes are placed in a container which is then filled with carbon dioxide gas to exclude air. After the bunches of grapes have been stored under these conditions for a number of days, they are crushed, yeast is added and a normal fermentation with short skin contact time is conducted. The aromas and flavours produced during the carbonic maceration stage become mixed with those of the normal fermentation, and this produces a more interesting wine.

In the mid 1980s the process was taken up by Australian winemakers to produce attractively coloured and fruity light reds from the varieties Shiraz, Cabernet Sauvignon and Grenache. Again Australian innovation came to the fore: a young Australian winemaker, the late Stephen Hickinbotham, developed a system which greatly improved the handling of grapes during the initial storage period. The grapes are picked by hand and placed directly into plastic bags packed into specially designed boxes. All this occurs in the vineyard. This way there is little damage to the berries and they remain intact. The boxes are transported back to the winery and stored for up to two weeks, allowing the carbonic maceration process to take place inside the berries. The grapes are then crushed and fermented on skins for a short period. The final result is a light, flavoursome red wine. This innovation was patented as the Cab Mac Process, and wines made by this method are labelled as Cab Mac. Mitchelton Winery in Victoria now has the rights to this name and the 'Cab Mac' label may only be used by this company.

In the classical method, as practised in France, the bunches of grapes are placed in large fermentation vessels for storage. However, the weight of the bunches crushes some of the grapes at the bottom, producing juice, and some normal fermentation can occur during the storage period. This is referred to as partial carbonic maceration. The innovation of storing the bunches in small boxes ensures that the berries remain intact during storage and that a full carbonic maceration occurs.

In practice, winemakers normally process some of the grapes by the carbonic maceration process, some by partial carbonic maceration and others by normal fermentation. The final wine is made up of a blend of these components.

Rosé and Cab Mac style wines are light-bodied wines, but there are also other wines which fit this category. Generally, light-bodied red wines can be made from a number of varieties, including Shiraz, Cabernet Sauvignon, Grenache and Pinot Noir. They can be made in different ways, some by fermenting the grapes for only a short time on skins, others by the carbonic maceration process or modifications of it, while others can be made by a normal fermentation procedure. Any batch of grapes with low levels of colour and tannins, regardless of the production technique, is likely to produce a lighter bodied wine as long as the alcohol level is not excessively high.

Enjoy rosé and light-bodied red wines slightly chilled. These are perfect summer luncheon wines.

Some examples of light-bodied red wines to try:

$\mathcal{P}$inot Noir

Pinot Noir is a grape variety that does not naturally develop high levels of colour and tannins and thus is more likely to produce light- to medium-bodied wines. Once this is realised, you can start to appreciate, as the French would say, 'the personality of the wine'. Pinot Noir wines have many rewarding taste sensations: an interesting array of primary and developed fruit characters, and, in the best wines, a mouthfeel that rivals the experiences that are found in the bigger wines from Cabernet Sauvignon and Shiraz.

Pinot Noir is a difficult variety 'to get right', both in the vineyard and the winery. There is a small but growing group of Australian winemakers who have taken up the Pinot challenge. Some makers will use the whole bunch fermentation technique, where the grapes are picked and placed in a tank under gas cover for a few days prior to crushing. Crushing is sometimes carried out by treading and breaking the grapes with the feet. The fermentation progresses gradually as the juice is released; it is essentially partial carbonic maceration.

Other makers crush the grapes, removing the stalks in the process, but then add back varying proportions of stalks to the must. Others use various combinations of whole bunches and crushed grapes. Some drain off a portion of the juice prior to fermentation; the flavours, colour and tannins extracted from the skins are then concentrated in the smaller volume of wine obtained. Often a batch of grapes is processed in several different ways to give the winemaker greater blending options in preparing the final wine.

The ferments are typically conducted at higher temperatures (often about 25 to 30ºC). These conditions aid in the extraction of colour and tannins, as well as inducing further complexity in the finished wine. After, and sometimes towards the end of, fermentation the wines are transferred to oak barrels, normally of French origin. This incorporates barrel ferment influence as well as oak characters; these add complexity but they should not be a major feature. It is the fruit characters that give these wines their personalities, those fresh raspberry, violet, plum-like primary fruit aromas and flavours, interwoven with the intriguing earthy, gamey, and barnyard-like sensations that develop with time.

SENSORY FEATURES OF PINOT NOIR WINES

APPEARANCE

The colour can vary from cherry red to plum red through to brown tones in older wines. The depth of colour is only light to medium compared to wines made from Cabernet Sauvignon or Shiraz.

AROMAS AND FLAVOURS

Primary fruit characters include *strawberry, red cherry, raspberry, black cherry, violet, plum, stewed plum, rhubarb, beetroot, blackcurrant* and *prune.*

Developed fruit characters include *earthy, cowyard, barnyard, gamey, bacon fat, mushroom* and *truffle.*

Characters derived from winemaking include

barrel fermentation/barrel storage - *spicy, coconut, smoky, chocolate* and *mocha.*

carbonic maceration - *spicy, cinnamon* and *fruity.*

addition of whole bunches/stalks - *stemmy, hay-like* and *stalky.*

THE PALATE

Flavours should be rich and mouth filling. The palate should highlight 'the Pinot feel' - a sappy, almost velvety impression in the mouth, with low to medium intensity of grainy tannins. The wine should finish with freshness, flavour persistence and softness.

Pinot Noir styles vary from light-bodied wines with more strawberry and red cherry-like characters through to wines with more body and a higher intensity of raspberry, plum, stewed plum and characters towards the riper end of the flavour spectrum. Generally, these medium-bodied styles are more complex, have more tannin and give that 'sappy' sensation on the palate.

The characters derived from winemaking may be present to varying degrees in the different styles. Carbonic maceration characters are more likely to be obvious in the lighter styles. Any stalky or oak characters should not dominate the expression of the primary and/or developed fruit.

$\mathcal{E}$xcellent Pinot Noir wines are produced in a number of our wine regions. It is a style of wine where there has been vast improvement in quality over recent years.

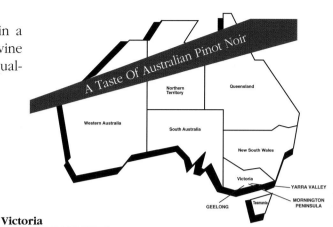

A Taste Of Australian Pinot Noir

South Australia

Adelaide Hills
Knappstein
Henschke
Pibbin
Hillstowe
Ashton Hills

Eden Valley
Mountadam

Coonawarra
Rouge Homme

Western Australia

Margaret River
Leeuwin
Moss Wood
Capel Vale

Great Southern
Wignalls

Victoria

Yarra Valley
Diamond Valley
Coldstream Hills
Long Gully
Shantell
De Bortoli
Tarrawarra
Yarra Burn
Yarra Ridge
Yarra Yering
Yerringburg

Gippsland
Bass Phillip
Wa-De-Lock
Nicholson River

Ovens Valley
Giaconda

Grampians
Best's Great Western
Montara
Seppelt

Mornington Peninsula
Dromana
Hickinbotham
Main Ridge
Moorooduc
Paringa
Stoniers

Geelong
Bannockburn
Scotchman's Hill
Prince Albert

Macedon
Rochford

New South Wales

Hunter Valley
Tyrrell's

Mudgee
Thistle Hill

Tasmania

North East
Pipers Brook
Delamere
Rochecombe

Central East Coast
Freycinet

South East
Moorilla
Meadowbank
Bream Creek

Pinot Noir wines, depending on their styles, can complement cold meats, pasta dishes, veal, lamb and a range of game such as duck and pheasant.

You will find a large group of Pinot Noir producers in the Yarra Valley, Mornington Peninsula and the Geelong area. These areas consistently produce quality Pinot Noir wines in a range of styles.

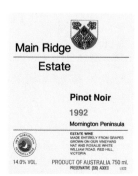

Main Ridge
Estate

Pinot Noir
1992
Mornington Peninsula

ESTATE WINE
MADE ENTIRELY FROM GRAPES
GROWN ON OUR VINEYARD
NAT AND ROSALIE WHITE
WILLIAM ROAD, RED HILL,
VICTORIA
14.0% VOL.   PRODUCT OF AUSTRALIA 750 ml.
PRESERVATIVE (220) ADDED

1989 MORNINGTON PENINSULA
PINOT NOIR

HICKINBOTHAM
HICKINBOTHAM WINEMAKERS PTY LTD
WILLIAMSTOWN VICTORIA
750ml WINE MADE IN AUSTRALIA 12.3% VOL

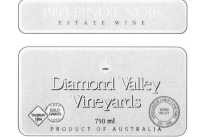

1993 PINOT NOIR
ESTATE WINE

Diamond Valley
Vineyards
750 ml
PRODUCT OF AUSTRALIA

BANNOCKBURN
GEELONG
Pinot Noir
1992   13.0% VOL
PRODUCE OF AUSTRALIA
750 ml

Medium- to full-bodied red wines

Medium- to full-bodied red wines are made from the varieties Cabernet Sauvignon, Shiraz, Cabernet Franc, Merlot, Malbec, Mataro, Durif and sometimes Pinot Noir and Grenache.

The making of these wines incorporates all the winemaking philosophies that were discussed under the section on red winemaking. The type of fruit the winemaker has to work with largely determines the temperature of fermentation, how the skins are worked (eg, pumped over or plunged), the length of time on skins and the use of barrel storage techniques.

Medium-bodied styles are normally made from grapes with sugar levels around 12º Baumé, by fermenting at about 20ºC, with moderate skin contact time, some pressings added to the free run, and oak storage.

Full-bodied styles are usually made from grapes with higher sugar levels (about 13º Baumé or more), with higher fermentation temperatures (about 25ºC), more working of the cap, longer skin contact time, a higher proportion of the pressings added to the free run, and oak storage.

After fermentation is complete, some winemakers leave the skins in contact with the finished wine. This allows more time for extraction of tannins from the skins and seeds, which helps to stabilise the colour of the wine as well as altering the overall structure of the tannins. The taste of the tannins is modified and they may appear less astringent and softer in the mouth, improving the mouthfeel of the wine overall.

Fermenting and/or storing the wine in oak barrels can also alter the taste of the wine, an aspect discussed earlier in the winemaking section. Often new oak barrels are used. Achieving the right balance of fruit flavours and oak characters is critical. Winemakers become experienced in assessing the impact of oak on different styles of wine and its potential effect on the flavours of the wine with time. Often different batches of wine will be left in oak for varying lengths of time, providing more options when the wines are blended.

Barrel positioning during storage is another variable used in making wines from varieties such as Cabernet Sauvignon and Shiraz. After the barrel

is filled with wine, it is either left with the bung at the twelve o'clock position or it is shived and rolled slightly so that the bung is at the two o'clock position.

Twelve o'clock position
When the barrel is stored in this position it can be frequently topped to compensate for evaporation losses. Each time the barrel is topped with wine some oxygen may be dissolved in the wine, which modifies the maturation process and creates a more complex wine with altered tannins.

Two o'clock position
When the barrel is in this position it does not require frequent topping. There is less oxygen pick-up and thus maturation reactions are minimised. The wine retains more primary fruit characters.

Wines may be stored in barrels for up to two years (or more). During this time oak characters are extracted from the barrel to different degrees depending upon the age of the barrels. The aromas, flavours, colours and tannins are modified as the wine slowly matures in the barrel. Wines are stored in either French or American oak barrels. French oak barrels are used more frequently for Cabernet Sauvignon as many winemakers consider that their oak aromas and flavours marry harmoniously with the weight and flavours of this variety. Shiraz wines are more often stored in American oak barrels.

Cabernet Sauvignon and Cabernet Sauvignon blends

Cabernet Sauvignon is considered by many to produce the ultimate taste in red wine. It can produce wines that are medium- to full-bodied with powerful flavours and great structure and is often blended with other varieties.

In wines from Cabernet Sauvignon grapes grown in cold to cool climates, the varietal aromas and flavours are often quite herbaceous and capsicum-like. These characters are most pronounced in wines that come from vines grown in cold to cool sites, with high yields and shaded canopies. Manipulation of the vine's canopy through improved trellising and/or practices such as removing leaves around bunches to expose the bunches to sunlight, can lessen the intensity of these characters, but generally Cabernet Sauvignon is not particularly suited to these colder sites. Often, even if the vines are well managed, the wines are high in acid, low in alcohol, colour and body and excessively herbaceous.

Grapes grown in cool to warm and warm conditions have mainly mint, berry and blackcurrant characters. Not only do wines made from these grapes normally have more colour and tannins but the tannins are also more finely structured.

Wines from grapes grown in hot conditions and with sound vine management generally have attractive berry characters but often have less intensity of flavour and colour than wines from warm regions.

Some wines made from Cabernet Sauvignon have a structure which winemakers call 'a hollow centre' or 'a doughnut effect'. In these wines the flavour is obvious when the wine enters the mouth and on the finish but lacks depth in the middle of the palate. Often winemakers blend Cabernet Sauvignon with other varieties to improve the weight of the middle palate and to soften the impact of the tannins. Many of the great Cabernet wines of the world are in fact blends. Merlot produces a less tannic wine than Cabernet Sauvignon and thus, on blending with Cabernet Sauvignon, can lessen the impact of the tannins. Merlot, as well as contributing its own varietal characters to the blend, also gives a more rounded mouthfeel.

Shiraz wines are also blended with Cabernet Sauvignon to fill out the middle palate, and to add richness and strength to the blend. This has become a classic Australian red wine blend to produce a range of wine styles.

What you will see on the label

Wines labelled Cabernet Sauvignon contain 85% or more of wine made from Cabernet Sauvignon grapes. When the proportion of Merlot or Shiraz is greater than 15%, the wine is labelled as Cabernet Sauvignon-Merlot or Cabernet Sauvignon-Shiraz, as the case may be. Sometimes Cabernet Sauvignon-Shiraz blends will be labelled Cabernet-Shiraz, but the former is more correct.

In other cases where the wine is a blend of a number of varieties, all the varieties may be shown on the label or the wine may be labelled as a 'brand name' for example Orlando Jacob's Creek, Mildara Jamieson's Run and Lindemans Pyrus.

Some of these wines are labelled 'Claret', a generic term used in Australia usually to describe a medium- to full-bodied red wine with a firm finish. With time this term will disappear from labels of Australian wine.

Coonawarra and McLaren Vale in South Australia, Margaret River in Western Australia and the Yarra Valley in Victoria produce some of Australia's best Cabernet Sauvignon and Cabernet Sauvignon blends.

Some wines are made from single vineyards and these wines highlight the particular characteristics of the soil and climate of that site. Other wines are made from a blend, often from different varieties and different vineyards. The flexibility to blend different wines gives our winemakers the opportunity to craft a wine of a desired style and quality.

$\mathscr{A}$ feature of Cabernet Sauvignon is its potential to age. Wines with abundant flavours and tannins and with balanced acidity can mature in the bottle for many years. A number of wineries release a wine as a young wine but hold some stock back for release when the wine is older. This offers the winemakers an opportunity to demonstrate the features of the style of their wine as both a young and a mature wine.

Also, some producers will hold a portion of the wine in oak storage for a longer period of time and release two wines from the same vintage. These special wines are often labelled 'Reserve Wines'. Some examples are Virgin Hills Reserve and Moss Wood Reserve.

Other producers use the word 'Reserve' for special blends. The word 'Reserve' often indicates that this is the producer's highest quality wine of that style.

A tasting experience

• Woodstock in the McLaren Vale region of South Australia is one winery where you can experience wines of two ages. Expect these wines either to show the rich blackcurrant flavours of young Cabernet Sauvignon; or these characters intermingled with the dusty, cigar-box and coffee features that develop with age, giving a complex older wine with mellowed tannins.

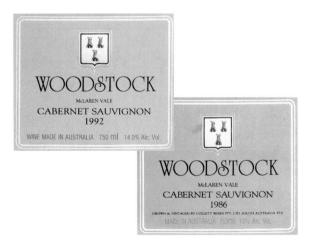

• Penfolds Bin 707 is one of Australia's most famous Cabernet Sauvignon wines. It is a blend of Cabernet Sauvignon grapes from Coonawarra and the Barossa Valley. Bin 707 is a wine with rich, concentrated ripe varietal characters combined with American oak influence, a wine with structure and strength to age for many years.

SENSORY FEATURES OF CABERNET SAUVIGNON WINES

APPEARANCE

The colour can vary from intense red with purple tinges in young wines through to brick red as the wine matures and finally to the brown colours of aged wine.

AROMAS AND FLAVOURS

Primary fruit characters include
capsicum, herbaceous, cinnamon, menthol, eucalyptus, leafy, minty, violet, perfumed, dusty, berry, stewed rhubarb, cooked beetroot, blackcurrant (cassis), black olive, licorice and *inky.*

Developed fruit characters include
earthy, dusty, cigar-box, licorice, chocolate, tobacco, coffee and *mocha.*

Characters derived from winemaking include barrel fermentation/barrel storage - *spice, coconut, smoky, chocolate, vanilla, pencil shavings, sawdust, toast, cedar, black olives, bacon, dusty, nuts, cashew, burnt* and *toffee.* Sometimes volatile acidity may be present.

THE PALATE

These wines vary from moderately flavoured and tannic, medium-bodied styles through to strongly flavoured and tannic, medium- to full-bodied styles. The flavours present in any particular wine depend on what flavours were present in the grapes, how the wine was made and the age of the wine.

The tannins impart firm astringency to the palate. Young wines with large amounts of tannin can give a furry sensation in the mouth. As the wine ages, the impact of the tannins diminishes and the tannins, especially in the better wines, give a fine grainy feeling in the mouth. Most of these wines have been stored in oak barrels and oak characters may be present on the nose and palate. Such characters should be well-integrated with the other features of the wine. French or American oak barrels are usually used for maturing these wines.

An 'apparent sweetness' may be perceived on the palate. This may come from the developed 'ripe' fruit characters and/or glycerol and/or alcohol. This impression may be more obvious in older wines.

The better wines have great balance, freshness and persistency of flavour, irrespective of their age.

A tasting experience

YELLOW LABEL

GREY LABEL

BLACK LABEL

T H E   G R A P E S

A blend of Cabernet Sauvignon, Shiraz and Merlot, sourced from a range of vineyards in South Australia.

A blend of Cabernet Sauvignon (80%) and Shiraz (20%), sourced from selected Langhorne Creek vineyards.

A blend of varieties from selected vineyards: Cabernet Sauvignon (about 75%) from Langhorne Creek and Clare, Merlot from Langhorne Creek and McLaren Vale vineyards and Shiraz from Eden Valley.

T H E   W I N E M A K I N G

The techniques at Wolf Blass Wines epitomise the skill of winemakers in recognising characters of different wines, either during fermentation or in the finished wines; through experience they select those wines with special characters for the desired styles and then through skilful blending craft the wines that represent the different labels. The fermentation technique is similar for these wines (Fermentation temperature is around 20ºC and with frequent mixing of the cap with the fermenting wine. The wines are taken off skins and pressed at about 4º Baumé); the major determinant of style comes from the characters in the grapes from the different vineyards and how the wine is handled towards the end, and after, fermentation.

The ferments are pressed and allowed to finish in stainless steel tanks. The wines are stored in new, 1 and 2 year old American and French oak barrels for a minimum of 12 months maturation.

The ferments from the individual vineyards are checked and those with intensity of eucalypt/mint characters are selected to finish their fermentation in new American and French oak barrels. The free run and press fractions are kept separate at this stage. After several rackings, final selections are made, the wine blended and placed in the same barrels for 24 months maturation.

Initial selection, on intensity of rich fruit characters, occurs during fermentation of the different wines. After pressing free run and press fractions complete their fermentation in brand new American and French oak barrels. The free run and press fractions are kept separate at this stage. After racking, the wines showing excellent fruit qualities, complexity and structure are settled, blended and stored in new oak barrels for a minimum of 24 months maturation.

T H E   T A S T E   O F   T H E   W I N E

Medium red in colour. Rich berry fruit and vanillin oak are obvious on the nose. A medium-bodied wine with spice and berry fruit flavours. Oak characters add to the complexity on the palate. A full flavoured wine with a soft tannin finish. A wine that is ready to be enjoyed now or cellar for a few years.

The wine is rich red. The nose shows spice and mint characters with integrated vanillin oak. The minty characters are typical of Langhorne Creek Cabernet Sauvignon. A full-bodied style with rich palate showing mint, berry and some developed chocolate flavours, with a firm tannin finish. A wine that will age well for 5-10 years or more.

Deep vibrant red colour. Complex and intense nose and palate showing blackcurrant, plum, mint, chocolate, earthy and smoky oak characters, all superbly integrated. A richly flavoured, full-bodied wine with plenty of supple tannins. A wine with great structure and will age well for 10 years or more.

Quality, reliable and affordable.

A crafted quality product, select grapes and skilful winemaking.

Premium quality, the pursuit of excellence.

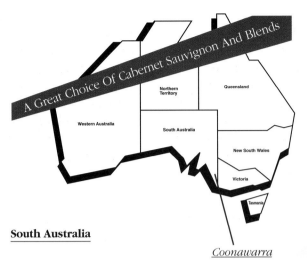

You will find good Cabernet Sauvignon wines and/or blends of various styles from all our wine producing regions. There are numerous producers and the selection below gives a guide to some of these producers in the various regions.

Western Australia

Margaret River
Well established Margaret River producers such as Cullens, Leeuwin Estate, Vasse Felix, Sandalford, Evans and Tate, Moss Wood and Cape Mentelle have an enviable reputation for their Cabernet Sauvignon wines.

Quality wines are also being produced from other wineries of Western Australia such as Killerby, Wrights, Chateau Xanadu, Devil's Lair, Goundrey, Howard Park and Plantagenet.

Victoria

Yarra Valley
Classic examples of Cabernet Sauvignon and/or blends come from the Yarra Valley from producers such as Mount Mary, Oakridge, Seville, Yarra Yering and Yeringberg. Many more recently established wineries in the Yarra Valley and Mornington Peninsula regions are producing wines that make the choice of quality Cabernet Sauvignon even greater. A few to try include Dromana, Main Ridge and Coldstream Hills.

Western Victoria
The regions around Bendigo, Ballarat, Avoca and Kyneton are the source of some of Australia's premium wines from Cabernet Sauvignon and blends, including Virgin Hills, Redbank, Mt Avoca, Taltarni and Dalwhinnie.

New South Wales

Hunter Valley
One of the most notable Cabernet Sauvignon wines from this region is Lake's Folly.

Mudgee
Fine Cabernet Sauvignon wines come from a number of producers. The wines from Huntington Estate and Montrose are good examples to try.

South Australia

Reynella / McLaren Vale / Langhorne Creek
These regions, just south of Adelaide, are well known for the quality of their wines from Cabernet Sauvignon and blends. There are many producers including Wirra Wirra, Hardys, Woodstock, Coriole, Chapel Hill, Ingolby, d'Arenberg, Temple Bruer and Pirramirra.

Clare
The wineries of the Clare region produce some top wines from this variety. Some to try include Leasingham, Taylors, Wendouree, Grosset, Sevenhills and Tim Adams.

Adelaide Plains
Here you will find Primo Estate's Joseph, an innovative Cabernet Sauvignon/Merlot wine produced by the amarone method where the grapes are partially dried before crushing to concentrate their flavours.

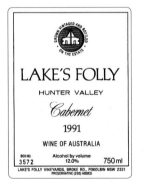

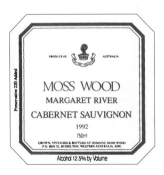

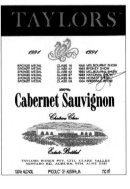

Coonawarra is Australia's most famous red wine producing region and it is here that you discover some of the best Cabernet Sauvignon wines, not only in Australia but in the world. Coonawarra has earned its reputation over many years, with great wines consistently produced by many of the wineries that make up this small but special vineyard area. Many wineries located in other parts of Australia also source grapes from this premium area.

Coonawarra cellar door sales outlets

Balnaves	Bowen Estate
Brand's Laira	Highbank
Hollick	Haselgrove
Katnook Estate	Ladbroke Grove
Leconfield	Majella
Mildara	Parker Estate
Lindemans	Penley Estate
Penowarra	Redman
Rouge Homme	Rymill
The Ridge	Wetherall
Wynns	Zema Estate

ADELAIDE 400km ↑

BRAND'S LAIRA

COONAWARRA

LINDEMANS

MILDARA

KATNOOK ESTATE

LECONFIELD

BOWEN ESTATE

BALNAVES

HOLLICK

PENOLA

MELBOURNE 420km ↘

Cabernet Sauvignon wines match a large range of full-flavoured foods including duck, game, lamb and beef.

$\mathcal{B}$lends of wines from different varieties and regions

As previously mentioned, many Australian red wines are a blend of two, three or more varieties. Australian winemakers are free to blend grapes from different varieties and from many areas. The wines are blended to improve the taste of the wine and/or to produce a consistency of style.

Blending is used in the making of expensive wines, as well as those at lower price points. Many of the wines we introduce to you in the section on Cabernet Sauvignon are blends. These include some of Australia's premium wines.

Blending is also used to produce Australia's top selling red wines. Without the freedom and opportunity to select grapes of different varieties and from different regions and then to blend the resulting wines, it would not be possible to obtain the volumes, quality and consistency of style that these wines represent. Among these wines are the well known *brand names*, labels such as Orlando Jacob's Creek, Penfolds Koonunga Hill, Tyrrells Long Flat Red, Wolf Blass Yellow Label, Mildara Jamieson Run, Peter Lehmann Clancy and Hardys Nottage Hill.

These are consistently well made, generously flavoured, easy drinking and affordable wines.

Red wine styles - a choice for every palate

In addition to the varieties already described, Australian vineyards also have plantings of Mataro, Grenache, Merlot, Cabernet Franc, Ruby Cabernet, Malbec, Durif, Tarrango, Chambourcin, Pinot Meunier, Zinfandel, Touriga, Graciano, Barbera and Sangiovese, some of which are grown in only small quantities.

Merlot

A large amount of the Merlot grown in Australia is incorporated into Cabernet Sauvignon blends. Merlot, as well as providing its own flavour profile characteristics, also gives a softening effect on the palate. Many producers are now increasing the proportion of Merlot in the blend, and these wines are labelled Cabernet Sauvignon Merlot. Some producers make a varietal Merlot, ie, a wine where the Merlot component is 85% or more, and often 100%. These wines typically have rounded tannins, coupled with plenty of berry and plum-like flavours and a fresh acid finish. Normally these wines have been stored in oak, adding further complexity to the taste of the wine. Some descriptors used for the primary fruit characters of Merlot include *herbaceous, fruity, aromatic, perfumed, violets, sappy, spicy, cherry, raspberry, plum, blackcurrant, mulberry, rhubarb* and *fruitcake*. Developed characters are similar to those of Cabernet Sauvignon.

Some examples to try:

South Australia
Irvine, Petaluma, Clarendon Hills

Western Australia
Evans and Tate, Cape Mentelle

Victoria
Mitchelton, Warrenmang
Yarra Yering

Mitchelton's Chinaman's Bridge Merlot.

Blends of Shiraz, Grenache and Mataro

The Rhône Valley in southern France has traditionally produced wines from Shiraz and a blend of Shiraz and other varieties. A typical blend is predominantly Shiraz, Grenache and Mourvedre (in Australia Mourvedre is also known as Mataro). Australia has considerable plantings of these varieties, and more winemakers are now again producing wines made from various blends of these three varieties, often from old, low yielding vines. These styles are now coming back into vogue.

Typically these wines have a range of characters often described as *spice, pepper, cherry, berry, plum, stewed plum, prune* and *licorice*. The types of characters present in any particular wine, and their intensity, depend on the proportion of each variety in the blend. These wines can develop very complex aromas and flavours, as a result of the developed *earthy, chocolate, gamey* and *barnyard* characters which appear with age. The palate can be richly textured, with apparent sweetness and soft tannins. Often the alcohol levels are relatively high, a feature that contributes to their full-bodied nature; oak need not be a feature.

These wines are a great accompaniment to mediterranean style foods. Expect to see a lot more of these wines in the future.

Some producers include:

Burge Family Winemakers, Veritas, Charles Melton, d'Arenberg, Mitchelton, Turkey Flat, Rockford, Penfolds and Yalumba.

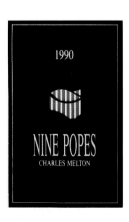

Durif

Durif is also a Rhône Valley variety. In Australia it is mainly planted in the north-east region of Victoria. It produces wines with intense colour, abundant spicy, plum fruit flavours and plenty of tannins, wines that have longevity and require cellaring. Seek out these wines at Campbell's, Fairfield, Stanton and Killeen and Morris wineries, all of which are in the Rutherglen area of Victoria.

Chambourcin

Chambourcin is a French hybrid but its parentage is unknown. John Cassegrain of Cassegrain Winery in Port Macquarie experimented with this variety in the early 1980s. Following its success in producing attractive, medium-bodied red wines with distinctive flavours, larger plantings have been established in the Hastings Valley, near Port Macquarie, NSW. It has good disease resistance and Cassegrain Winery is now developing a totally organic vineyard planted predominantly with Chambourcin.

Cassegrain Chambourcin is a medium-bodied wine, normally crimson coloured, with *spicy, peppery* fruit characters and a soft finish. Usually a component of the wine is made by partial carbonic maceration techniques.

The Italian varieties

There is now an increasing interest in the varieties that originate from the Italian wine regions, varieties such as Sangiovese, Barbera and Nebbiolo. Sangiovese and Barbera are usually used to make light- to medium-bodied wines with mainly raspberry-like flavours, while Nebbiolo normally can make intensely flavoured (*violet, plum, prune, licorice*) wines with high levels of tannin. The quantities of wine currently produced from these varieties are not large, but in the future expect to see the names of these varieties on more bottles of Australian wine.

Some examples to try:

Coriole Sangiovese from the McLaren Vale region of South Australia.

Brown Brothers Barbera from Milawa in Victoria.

Shiraz

Vines from the variety Syrah were planted in the Rhône Valley of France hundreds of years ago. It is here that Syrah and its wines have become famous, a reputation established over many years. In Australia Syrah is known as Shiraz. Australia is the only other country with significant plantings of this variety and in less than two hundred years has also built an enviable reputation for quality Shiraz wines. Shiraz has the versatility to adapt to a range of climates, and generously flavoured and complex wines can be found across our grapegrowing regions.

Grown in cooler climates, Shiraz grapes typically produce wines with distinctive pepper and spice tones, along with berry fruit characters. Wines from grapes grown in warmer climates may show blackberry, mulberry, plum, as well as spice and earthy characters. Further, in warmer climates, wines from well managed vines (and where the grapes ripen to sugar levels around 13° Baumé or more) can have plum, stewed plum, licorice and chocolate types of aromas and flavours. At this stage of ripening the grapes may start to shrivel, and it is a finely balanced stage in the ripening process. Picked 'at just the right time' these grapes can produce wonderful, full-bodied, richly flavoured and textured wines. If grapes are left too long on the vine, these rich characters may change and the overwhelming sensation can be a jammy character. Grapes grown in hotter climates typically produce wines with more raspberry but also with blackberry and plum characters. The intensity of flavour and colour is generally not as strong as in wines from warm climates.

The intensity of flavours depends very much on the vineyard management practices. Lower yielding vines with well managed canopies and irrigation scheduling can often produce grapes with concentrated flavours, giving wine with rich, intense and complex tastes. These vineyards receive little or no irrigation and are often referred to as 'dry-land' grown.

Shiraz wines are made in a variety of ways, but generally with techniques that give medium to high extraction of colour and flavour from the skins. The big full-bodied styles will probably have been 'worked a lot more' (pumped over, plunged etc) in their making. Most wines will be matured in American oak. The power of each seems to be well matched, and thus some wines may show vanillin and other oak characters along with their intense berry flavours.

SENSORY FEATURES OF SHIRAZ WINES

APPEARANCE

The colour of young wines varies from medium red through to intensely rich purple/red, almost black, in the bigger wine styles. As these wines mature, they progress through various shades and intensities of red to the red brown and then the distinctly tawny colour of age.

AROMAS AND FLAVOURS

Primary fruit characters include
herbs, mint, spice, pepper, menthol, eucalypt, raspberry, dark cherry, mulberry, blackberry, plum, blackcurrant, black olives, aniseed, licorice, stewed plum, chocolate, jammy and *raisin.*

Developed fruit characters include
chocolate, earthy, barnyard, cowyard, cigar-box, coffee, gamey, meaty, salami, savoury and *leather.*

THE PALATE

These wines generally have plenty of flavour, often with a mid-palate sweetness from ripe fruit and/or high alcohol. Interesting complexity comes with time, as the primary fruit characters slowly change to subtle earthy, chocolate, barnyard expressions.

Most wines give a firm tannin impression on the palate, which varies from big, but soft, chewy and mouth-puckering sensations in young wines, to a more grainy feeling in older wines. Some wines will be high in alcohol (greater than 13%v/v) and may impart a spicy, hot feeling at the back of the mouth when swallowed. However, these higher alcohol levels are often not as obvious in well flavoured and balanced wines, with the fruit intensity well able to handle such levels of alcohol.

Oak characters may be incorporated in the flavour, structure and maturation of these wines. Full-bodied styles can absorb more oak influence; however in any wine, either medium- or full-bodied in style, the oak characters should be well integrated with the other features of the wine.

Quality red wines, whatever their style, should express a balance of flavours, acid, tannins, oak and alcohol.

Shiraz

Victoria

Some of the Australia's best cool climate Shiraz wines come from western and central Victoria. Typically these wines are intensely flavoured, showing a range of characters including spice, pepper, berry fruits and plum. The cooler the climate the more obvious are the spice and pepper characters. Generally, the tannin levels are moderate to high and finely structured and have a lovely, soft feel in the mouth.

There are many wineries to visit including:

Knight's Granite Hills	Tisdall
Best's	Hanging Rock
Seppelt	Chateau Tahbilk
Craiglee	Mitchelton
Mount Langi Ghiran	Chateau Leamon
Balgownie	Heathcote
Passing Clouds	Taltarni
Jasper Hill	Harcourt Valley
Dalwhinnie	Water Wheel
Mount Avoca	Redbank

Vines were planted at Best's Concongella vineyard in 1866, and some still survive today as a living museum of the history that has passed through five generations of the Thomson family. Viv Thomson is the current custodian of this piece of Australian history. The old wooden slab winery that houses the cellar door sales area is a great place to savour not only their Shiraz but also wines from other varieties.

Craiglee is another winery steeped in history. Vines were first planted there in 1863, but were pulled out in 1928. The Carmody family replanted the vineyard in 1976. The wines of Craiglee and those of Trevor Mast of Mount Langi Ghiran winery have become benchmarks for cool climate Shiraz.

Wineries in the north-east region of Victoria are famous for their robust, full flavoured and tannic wines made from Shiraz, although now many are not as massive as they were in the past. Here you will find rich, full-bodied styles with spice, plum, blackberry and chocolate characters and stacked with soft, mouthfilling tannins. These wines come from wineries such as Stanton and Killeen, All Saints, Campbell's, Baileys, Morris and Chambers.

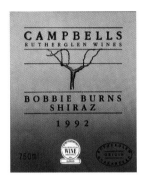

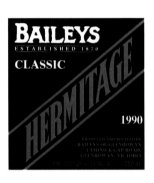

Full flavoured wines from this variety are also made by a number of new wineries in this north-eastern region, in a sub-region known as Ovens Valley, including Boynton's of Bright and Pennyweight.

New South Wales

The Hunter Valley has traditionally made medium- to full-bodied Shiraz wines with spice, raspberry and plum characters. As these wines mature, characteristic regional earthy tones develop. Generally these wines have complex, rich flavours and a soft tannic finish. They come from wineries such as Tyrrell's, Lindemans, Pepper Tree, Rothbury, Brokenwood, McGuigan Brothers and Arrowfield.

Vineyards are being established in new regions of New South Wales including the areas around Young, Orange and Forbes. New labels are constantly appearing.

McWilliams Barwang Shiraz; a cool climate style from newly established vineyards in the highlands near Young.

Queensland

Shiraz also performs well in the Granite Belt region. Wines from Mount Magnus, Ballandean and Bald Mountain are good examples to try.

Western Australia

Shiraz grapes grown in the Margaret River and Southern regions produce elegant medium- to full-bodied wines with complex, rich, spicy, peppery and ripe berry flavours and fine grained tannins.

Wines typical of this style are produced by:

Sandalford, Evans and Tate, Plantagenet, Pattersons, Chatsfield, Cape Mentelle, Killerby, Goundrey, Houghton.

South Australia

The flavours that we associate with Shiraz wines from Coonawarra are spice, pepper, plum, dark cherry, mulberry and blackberry, often complemented by oak characters. Older wines develop chocolate, coffee-like characters.

Some examples to try:

Wynns, Bowen Estate, Zema Estate, Hollick, Balnaves, Penley Estate.

The Padthaway region is known for the quality of its white wines, but some top Shiraz wines also come from this area. This is where the fruit for Orlando's Lawson and Hardys' Eileen Hardy Shiraz is sourced.

The McLaren Vale region, south of Adelaide, produces intensely flavoured, full-bodied Shiraz wines. These tend to have rich flavours of dark cherry, plum and licorice and plenty of firm, mouthfilling tannins. They soften with age, and as the earthy, gamey, barnyard developed characters build the wine becomes smooth and more complex on the palate. Some of these wines come from very old vines.

Some examples to try:

Chapel Hill   Pirramimma
Haselgrove   Cambrai
Wirra Wirra   Coriole
Andrew Garrett
d'Arenberg
Richard Hamilton
Woodstock
Kays
Seaview
Fern Hill

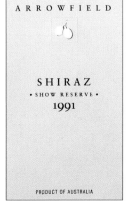

Wineries located in other areas also source grapes from this region, including Rosemount and Arrowfield, which are situated in the Hunter Valley of New South Wales.

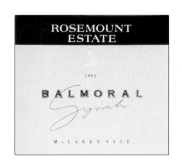

The Clare Valley also produces a range of wine styles from Shiraz that is well worth discovering. The wines range from the spicy, peppery styles through to the more full-bodied styles, crammed with flavour and tannins. Again some of these wines come from very old vines.

Some examples to try:

Mitchells   Pikes
Taylors   Sevenhills
Leasingham   Taylors
Waninga   Tim Adams
Jim Barry   Wendouree

Jim Barry Wines, just north of Clare, is the home of 'The Armagh' a complex wine with concentrated rich fruit and oak flavours.

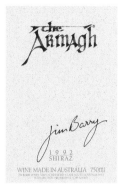

Wendouree is traditionally known for producing powerful red wines rich in flavours and tannins.

Old Shiraz vines are also grown in the Barossa Ranges. This is the source of Henschke's famous wines, Mount Edelstone and Hill of Grace.

Mount Edelstone is a wine rich in spice, pepper and plum characters, and with a long, soft tannin finish.

Hill of Grace is a warm, rich, complex, full-bodied wine with concentrated plum, blackberry, licorice and some spice characters and luscious tannins. One of Australia's most renowned and famous Shiraz wines.

The Barossa Valley is the home of rich, full-bodied Shiraz styles. In the warm Mediterranean climate, low yielding Shiraz vines, many well over 50 years old, ripen grapes with high sugar levels and packed with flavour, which produce intensely flavoured wines with spicy, plum, stewed plum and licorice characters. These wines develop earthy, chocolate complexity with age. Often they have been stored in new American oak barrels, and some oak characters may be evident.

Rockford's Basket Press Shiraz is one of the wines that highlights this style. Robert O'Callaghan of Rockford epitomises the spirit of many Barossa winemakers and their faith that these gnarled old Shiraz vines will give wines of character, an expression of the 'terroir' of the Barossa Valley.

As Robert O'Callaghan says, "The skill is in capturing and enhancing the fleeting flavours that grapes develop from their variety and extract from the earth, then bottling them as a living record of all that they represent."

St Halletts Old Block Shiraz comes from old blocks of Shiraz vines that are found from the southern edge of the Barossa to the Eden Valley. The integrity of each parcel of fruit is maintained throughout the winemaking process. After oak maturation all wines are tasted and those with the characteristics for Old Block are blended to be the wine for that vintage.

Peter Lehmann, Elderton, Veritas, The Willows, Charles Cimicky, Charles Melton, Wolf Blass Wines, Grant Burge, Kaesler and Penfolds are other wineries producing wines that express the character of the Barossa.

The Penfolds range of Shiraz wines begins with Bin 28 and progresses through to Grange. Today vines from the Barossa Valley provide the back-bone of many of these wines. The special char-acters of low yielding Shiraz vines and the skills that are used in crafting their grapes into wine are demonstrated to the full in the making of Grange, Australia's most famous wine.

Enjoy Shiraz wines with a range of full flavoured foods including lamb, beef and kangaroo.

A Collection Of Barossa Valley Shiraz

The Benefits Of Drinking Red Wine In Moderation

Research shows that drinking wine in small to moderate amounts can have significant health benefits, as well as providing enjoyment through its taste, especially when drunk with food.

Drinking wine will lower the risk of cardiovascular disease, including blood pressure, heart attacks and strokes, by:

- increasing the blood concentration of HDL - the 'good' cholesterol and oxidatively modifying LDL - the 'bad' cholesterol, and
- decreasing thrombosis (blood clotting).

Research also shows that people who drink wine in moderation (as opposed to those who do not drink wine or those who drink excessively) are likely to live longer (the 'French Paradox').

These and other benefits may be associated with phenolic substances found in wine. Red wines appear to be more beneficial because they contain higher amounts of these compounds.

Further information

A comprehensive coverage of wine and health issues is given in a booklet 'Wine and Health' authored by Dr Norrie, a wine author, historian, medical practitioner and vigneron. The booklet is available through McWilliam's Wines.

Further information can also be obtained from
Creina Stockley, Information Manager,
The Australian Wine Research Institute, Adelaide.

Wine And Health

A tasting experience

| KALIMNA BIN 28 | COONAWARRA BIN 128 | MAGILL ESTATE |

T H E   G R A P E S

Grapes are sourced from vineyards in the Barossa Valley (Kalimna), McLaren Vale, Langhorne Creek, Clare, Padthaway and Coonawarra.

Grapes are sourced from various vineyards across the Coonawarra region.

The grapes come from a single 6 ha vineyard (Magill Estate), in the eastern suburbs near the foothills of Adelaide. It is non-irrigated and the vines range in age from 30 to 50 years.

T H E   W I N E M A K I N G

The winemaking technique for both of these wine styles is similar. Grapes are crushed and transferred to stainless steel fermenters of 10 to 35 tonne capacity, fitted with heading-down boards. These boards hold the cap of skins and seeds (that rise during the fermentation) below the fermenting liquid, ensuring that the skins are always kept moist. The must is held at higher temperatures until fermentation commences and then the fermentation temperature is slowly dropped and maintained at about 20ºC. Throughout the fermentation the fermenting liquid is completely drawn off from the skins and then returned by spraying back through the boards and over the cap of skins (racked and returned). This procedure is carried out each day. Towards the end of fermentation the wine is pressed. On completion of fermentation the wine is racked. A blend is prepared from the various wines and then stored in oak barrels. Kalimna Bin 28 is matured in American oak barrels, at the twelve o'clock position, for an average period of 12 to 15 months. Coonawarra Bin 128 is stored in French oak barrels (20% new), at the twelve o'clock position for an average period of 15 months. All barrels are regularly topped. At the end of the storage period the wines from the different barrels of each wine style are separately blended.

Grapes are crushed and transferred to 6 tonne open fermenters with heading-down boards. The must is initially maintained at higher temperatures until fermentation commences and then dropped slowly to a fermentation temperature less than 20ºC. The wine is racked and returned daily. On completion of fermentation it is pressed, racked and then transferred to a combination of new American and French oak barrels at the twelve o'clock position for about 15 months.

T H E   T A S T E   O F   T H E   W I N E

The wine is medium-red coloured. and has warm, ripe berry (often mulberry) and smoky oak aromas. The palate is rich and flavoursome with sweet berry fruit, vanillin oak and solid tannins.

Medium-red colour. Lifted peppery, Coonawarra Shiraz varietal fruit and subtle French oak characters on the nose. Soft and complex palate, featuring a harmonious spicy fruit and dusty oak combination. Medium- to full-bodied the wine finishes with a soft, lingering tannin finish.

The wine is deep plum in colour. A complex bouquet featuring spicy Shiraz fruit characters and integrated oak. A more refined style compared to Penfolds traditional red wines; it displays rich and spicy Shiraz fruit and distinctive oak on the palate. A full flavoured, elegant structure and medium weight wine with great length and a soft tannin finish.

W I N E   S T Y L E

A firm, full-bodied, ripe Shiraz style. Can be enjoyed on release and should age well for at least 10 years.

Bin 128 captures the pepper and berry fruit regional characters of Shiraz from Coonawarra combined with subtle oak complexity. Enjoy on release or over a 10 year period.

An elegant crafted style, with potential to develop great complexity over a 10 to 15 year period.

Quality, reliable and affordable.

Quality, reliable and affordable.

A crafted quality product, select grapes and skilful winemaking.

GRANGE

T H E   G R A P E S

Grapes are sourced from a selection of premium low yielding South Australian vineyards, with Penfolds Kalimna vineyard and selected Barossa vineyards forming the backbone. Average yields are normally less than 5 tonnes per hectare.

▼

T H E   W I N E M A K I N G

Grapes are crushed and transferred to fermenters of 10 to 20 tonne capacity, fitted with heading-down boards. The must is initially maintained at higher temperatures until fermentation commences and then the temperature of fermentation does not exceed 25°C. The ferment is worked regularly, with the rack and returns (described on the opposite page) conducted daily. When the fermentation is nearly finished the wine is drawn off (free run) and the remaining mass of skins is transferred to the press. Each portion is transferred to new American oak barrels, where the fermentation is completed. This imparts barrel fermentation characters to the wine. After a short period on yeast lees in the barrel the wine is racked, blended and transferred back to new American oak barrels. The wines mature in these barrels, which are stored at the twelve o'clock position for 18 months or more. They are regularly racked and/or topped during this period to craft the required style and to expose it to some air, enhancing the maturation. After storage in barrel, the different barrels are tasted and the appropriate blend is assembled; only those wines with the flavour intensity and other characters of Grange are selected.

▼

THE   TASTE   OF   THE   WINE

The wine is intensely deep, red coloured as a young wine. The bouquet is complex featuring opulent, ripe Shiraz berry fruit characters, varying from spice, cherry and plum fragrances through to soft, earthy nuances combined with new barrel fermentation characters and vanillin oak complexity. A wine with firm astringency, balanced acidity and integrated distinctive oak features. A full-bodied, richly flavoured and complex wine with a sweet middle palate and with spice, berry fruit and ripe plum flavours complemented with plenty of mouth-filling tannins. The wine becomes more complex with time.

▼

W I N E   S T Y L E

A full-bodied wine, with intense, rich and complex flavours and tannins, structured with a capacity to develop in the bottle and mature over a long period of time. Most Granges develop superbly over a 20 year or more period.

**Premium quality,
the pursuit of excellence.**

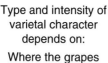

Type and intensity of
varietal character
depends on:

Where the grapes
were grown

How ripe the grapes
were at harvest

How the vines were
managed

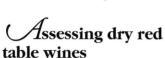

$\mathcal{A}$ssessing dry red table wines

Rosé styles should be light red/crimson and without orange tinges.

Other dry red table wines are various shades and intensities of red.

Young wines may show purple tinges.

Older wines develop red/brown and brown colours. In some wines, crystals of tartrate and sediments of colours and tannins may appear as the wine ages. These are not harmful and can be easily removed by decanting the wine prior to serving.

Wines may exhibit primary and/or developed fruit characters and in some wines other characters derived from winemaking.

Look for
- intensity and balance of characters
- complexity

Look for
- intensity and balance of characters
- pleasant mouthfeel sensations
- freshness
- balanced acidity
- richness/roundness
- complexity
- finesse and elegance
- persistent aftertaste
- the character of the tannins: supple, soft, pleasant, furry, grainy, not overly astringent

Examples of varietal character descriptors

The combination of descriptors will vary from wine to wine.

Pinot Noir:	**Primary fruit characters** strawberry, red cherry, raspberry, black cherry, violet, perfumed, plum, stewed plum, rhubarb, beetroot, sappy, blackcurrant, prune. **Developed fruit characters** earthy, cowyard, barnyard, gamey, bacon fat, mushroom, truffle.
Cabernet Sauvignon:	**Primary fruit characters** capsicum, herbaceous, cinnamon, menthol, eucalyptus, leafy, sappy, minty, violet, perfumed, dusty, berry, stewed rhubarb, cooked beetroot, blackcurrant (cassis), black olive, licorice, inky. **Developed fruit characters** earthy, dusty, cigar-box, licorice, chocolate, coffee, mocha.
Merlot:	**Primary fruit characters** herbaceous, fruity, aromatic, perfumed, violet, sappy, spice, cherry, plum, blackcurrant, mulberry, pumpkin, fruitcake. **Developed fruit characters** similar to Cabernet Sauvignon.
Grenache:	**Primary fruit characters** spice, cherry, raspberry, blackberry, plum, stewed plum, prune. **Developed fruit characters** earthy, barnyard, gamey.
Shiraz:	**Primary fruit characters** herbs, mint, spice, pepper, menthol, eucalypt, raspberry, dark cherry, mulberry, blackberry, plum, blackcurrant, black olives, aniseed, licorice, prune, stewed plum, chocolate, jammy, raisin. **Developed fruit characters** chocolate, earthy, barnyard, cowyard, cigar-box, coffee, gamey, meaty, salami, savoury, leather.

THE WINEMAKING PROCESS

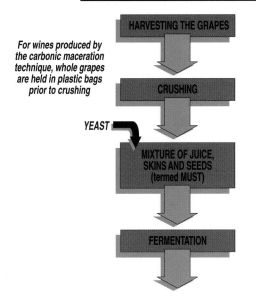

For wines produced by the carbonic maceration technique, whole grapes are held in plastic bags prior to crushing

HARVESTING THE GRAPES

CRUSHING

YEAST

MIXTURE OF JUICE, SKINS AND SEEDS (termed MUST)

FERMENTATION

DURING THIS PERIOD COLOUR, TANNINS AND FLAVOUR COMPOUNDS ARE EXTRACTED FROM THE SKINS

━━━ OPTIONS OF FERMENTATION TECHNIQUES ━━━

TIME ON SKINS	EXTRACTION METHOD	TEMPERATURE	TYPE OF FERMENTATION VESSEL	TYPE OF YEAST	BARREL FERMENTATION

A short time on skins produces lighter bodied styles eg Rosé or light reds

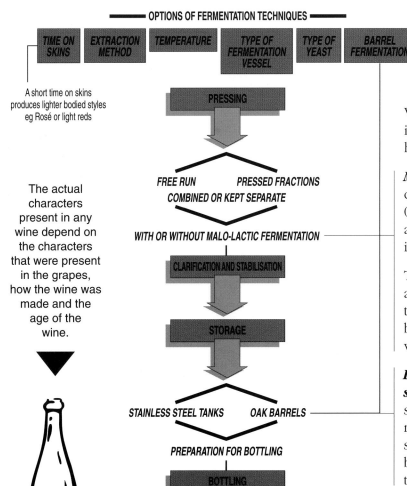

PRESSING

FREE RUN   PRESSED FRACTIONS
COMBINED OR KEPT SEPARATE

The actual characters present in any wine depend on the characters that were present in the grapes, how the wine was made and the age of the wine.

WITH OR WITHOUT MALO-LACTIC FERMENTATION

CLARIFICATION AND STABILISATION

STORAGE

STAINLESS STEEL TANKS   OAK BARRELS

PREPARATION FOR BOTTLING

BOTTLING

MATURATION IN THE BOTTLE

*O*ptimum temperature range for enjoying red wines:

about 15-18ºC; the higher end of the range is more appropriate for full-bodied styles.

Decanting

Red wines may need to be decanted to remove the wine from any deposits and to freshen up the wine. Some wines, and particularly older wines, may be subtly flavoured and excessive reaction with air may not be beneficial. Thus, decanting should be gentle and carried out immediately before serving the wine. If the wine requires further time to breathe it is best that this occurs in the glass where the wine's development can be more readily observed.

Wines that have partially fermented in or stored in oak barrels may have additional characters.

Malo-lactic fermentation (MLF)

creamy, buttery, yogurt, caramel. (Although these characters are not as obvious in red wines as they are in white wines.)

The lactic acid formed has a less acid taste than the malic acid, and the conversion thus results in a better acid balance in the wine; the wine tastes softer on the palate.

Barrel fermentation/barrel storage

spice, coconut, smoky, chocolate, mocha, vanilla, pencil shavings, sawdust, toast, cedar, black olives, bacon, dusty, nuts, cashew, burnt, toffee and caramel.

The alcohol level of these wines is usually between 11 and 14% alcohol by volume.

The solera system

A solera system is used for storing casks of wines of different ages. The oldest wines are stored in the bottom barrels and the youngest at the top. At various times of the year a quantity of wine is drawn off from the barrels on the bottom row of the solera. This portion of wine is then replaced with a younger wine from the next upper layer of barrels and so on.

This process of adding a portion of younger wine to older wine is called 'refreshing the wine'.

This system of storing wines can be used in the production of sherries, ports, muscats and tokays. This 'dynamic' ageing process of fractional blending ensures that the wine in the bottom barrels are of a consistent style and quality. It maintains freshness and consistency of 'house style'.

A solera system at McWilliam's Wines.

Fortified wine

The term 'fortified' is applied to wines that have had spirit added, raising the alcohol level of the finished wine to between 17 and 20% v/v; they include *sherry*, *port*, *muscat* and *tokay*. Sometimes you will see ports, muscats, tokays and the sweeter sherry styles referred to as dessert or fortified dessert wines.

The spirit added to the wine is either so-called SVR (at 95% v/v) or brandy spirit (at about 80% v/v). Apart from being a high strength alcohol solution, each has its own distinctive characters that it imparts to the finished wine. Makers of fortified wines normally have a preference for the type of spirit they add, depending on the style of fortified wine they intend to produce.

Australia produces some of the finest fortified wines in the world, including a unique, luscious, complex wine style that has developed in the north-eastern region of Victoria, known simply as *Muscat of Rutherglen.*

Fortified wines come in a range of types and styles. Sherries are normally used as an apéritif and enjoying their nutty, complex smells and tastes can create a relaxed atmosphere prior to the meal. Ports, muscats, tokays and the sweeter sherry styles are usually served towards the end of the meal, with rich desserts, cheeses and coffee. Fortified wines are wines to be sipped and savoured; relax and enjoy their complex and entrancing characters. Drinking these wines is essentially 'tasting history', since many come from blends where components may be 5, 10, 20, 50 and in some cases 100 years old.

Many fortified wines are assembled by way of a solera system.

The art of making fortified wines develops with experience, this often being passed down through generations. Try Australia's fortified wine styles and savour the taste of history.

For many Australians, the name McWilliam's means renowned ports and sherries, but like a number of producers based in the hotter vine-growing regions, McWilliam's have constantly explored new horizons and have developed vineyards and connections in traditional and new cool climate regions such as Coonawarra and Barwang. This allows McWilliam's to produce quality wines across a large range of wine types and styles. The same applies to other wineries, including those of the Rutherglen region which, although famous for their muscat and tokay wines, also produce a range of quality white and red table wine styles.

We mention this point because many of the producers of fortified wines are based in the warm to hot and hot regions, but that does not mean that they produce fortified wine styles exclusively. Appreciating that Australian wine companies produce wines from grapes grown not only in their immediate area but in many diverse vine-growing regions is part of understanding the Australian wine scene.

However, wine consumers are fortunate that companies like McWilliam's, Seppelt, Bullers, Campbells and Brown Brothers have maintained stocks of these old fortified wines from which they prepare wonderful blends of sherries, ports, muscats and tokays, so that not only our generation but those to come can enjoy these wine styles.

Sherry

Sherry is made from white grape varieties, normally Palomino and Pedro Ximines, and is made in three main styles, *Fino*, *Amontillado* and *Oloroso*.

How these wines are made

Fino style

The grapes are picked at about 10° Baumé and processed into a dry wine according to normal white wine making procedures. Spirit is added to the finished wine to increase the alcohol content to approximately 15.5% v/v and the wine is transferred to the upper stage of a solera. Sometimes the finished white wine is stored for a number of years before being fortified and transferred to the solera.

Each barrel in the solera is only partly filled with wine. The wine in each barrel is seeded with a special yeast strain called *flor* yeast and then stored in these barrels for a number of years. It is this stage of the production process that is critical in creating the unique character of fino and amontillado sherry. Because the barrels are only partly filled, the upper surface of the wine is exposed to air, providing conditions that are conducive to oxidation and to the growth of the flor yeast, which grows over the surface of the wine forming a film. The flor yeast develops and the wine matures during the years the wines are stored in the barrel. The chemical changes associated with the oxidation and the growth of the flor yeast impart new flavours to the wine.

During this period it is important to keep the conditions just right for the growth of the flor yeast: the surface must not be disturbed: the temperature must be kept between 15 and 20°C; and the alcoholic strength must be maintained at between 15.0 and 15.5% v/v. In a solera, where the wine is continuously refreshed, the flor growth continues almost indefinitely. The longer the wine spends on flor, the greater the development of nutty and almond-like characters. When

The flor yeast grows on top of the wine in a partially filled barrel.

the winemaker decides that the characters of the wines in the lower stages of the solera match the desired style, the wines are removed and blended, and further spirit is added to increase the alcohol content to about 18% v/v. The wine may then be stored for a further period of time in large barrels. These fino style sherries are not sweetened.

Normally wines spend from one to two years on flor, but special wines are kept in contact with the flor for up to seven years or more before being blended and bottled.

Amontillado style

This is initially made in the same way as fino sherries. An amontillado sherry has two distinct maturation periods, the first as a fino 'on flor' and then 'off flor' to develop into an amontillado style. Wines that have been stored in the 'fino solera' for a number of years are removed, fortified to 18% v/v alcohol and then transferred to a new solera stack specifically for amontillado style sherry. At this alcohol level no further flor growth occurs but the wine continues to mature; it becomes more golden in colour and fuller and richer on the palate.

Oloroso style

Oloroso styles of sherry should not be influenced by flor growth. They are produced by fortifying dry white wine to 18% v/v and then storing it in barrels or in a solera system for many years. Often the dry white wine has been produced from riper grapes with more fruity, aromatic characters.

Wines are stored in the oloroso solera for from 10 to 30 years or even more. They develop rich, complex flavours to complement the aromatic primary fruit characters. The longer they are stored, the more complex and rich they become. When removed from the solera they are normally sweetened before being bottled.

SENSORY FEATURES OF SHERRY

APPEARANCE

Fino sherry
pale straw, straw, pale gold.

Amontillado
golden, deep golden.

Oloroso
deep golden, golden amber with olive green tinges.

AROMAS AND FLAVOURS

Some words used to describe the characters that come from the flor and maturation are *nutty, almonds, walnuts, orange-peel, marmalade, aldehyde, oxidised, buttery, marzipan, caramel* and *rancio*.

Rancio is a difficult term to describe. It is used to describe the smell that comes from wines deliberately aged with some air contact and/or from wines that have spent a long time in oak casks. It encompasses *nutty, vanillin, almond, walnut* and *musty walnut*, and associated odours. It is a very positive feature and is a part of the character of fine sherries, ports, muscats, tokays and brandies.

THE PALATE

Fino sherries are the lightest in body and have the driest finish. They should be fresh and show distinctive aldehydic (nutty) characters.

Amontillado sherries are fuller and richer and show more aged characters (more rancio) than fino sherries. Although some sweetener may have been added prior to bottling they should finish dry.

Oloroso styles are the fullest, richest and most complex, fruity and aromatic and normally have higher alcohol content than flor sherries. Sweetener is added prior to bottling and they are semi-sweet to sweet full-bodied sherries.

What you will see on the label

These wines are labelled Fino, Amontillado or Oloroso Sherry. Often they have special names or codes, eg, Seppelt DP 117 Fino Sherry. Many are labelled as Show or Show Series, eg, McWilliam's or Seppelt Show Series, indicating that these are wines specially selected and blended for the wine show circuit but also available commercially in small volumes.

With time the name sherry will disappear from Australian wine labels; consumers will need to be familiar with special names and codes that identify Australian sherry style wines.

Some examples to try:

Seppelt	McWilliam's
Lindemans	Yalumba
Mildara	

A tasting experience

The best way to experience the distinctive characters of the different styles of sherry is to try the range from one producer, particularly their show series. All these wines have come from their separate soleras.

Seppelt Show Fino Sherry DP 117 is a blend of wines from Palomino grapes that have been 'on flor' for a minimum of 7 years and then further matured in large oak barrels for some months prior to bottling. The bouquet and flavours are intense, nutty and complex, showing classic flor character. The palate is fresh, the flavours lingering and the finish dry. Enjoy it slightly chilled.

Seppelt Show Amontillado Sherry DP 116 is a blend of wines from Palomino grapes, of an average age of 16 years. It shows excellent aged flor sherry characters with intense, complex and rich almond bouquet and flavours and a dry lingering finish. Enjoy it slightly chilled.

Seppelt Show Oloroso Sherry DP 38 comes from a blend of wines from Palomino and Grenache grapes which have an average age of 18 years. This wine shows rich, complex, ripe fruit, old oak and rancio characters. The palate is luscious but still has a drying finish.

Port

There are two main styles of port, *Tawny Port* and *Vintage Port*.

How these wines are made

Tawny port

The grape varieties normally used in the production of Australian tawny port are Shiraz, Grenache, Touriga and Mataro. The grapes are picked at about 15° Baumé; some berry shrivel normally occurs. Warm to hot climates are most suitable for growing grapes for port style wines, since the conditions are favourable for producing higher sugar levels as well as an intensity of flavours.

The grapes are crushed and fermented on skins to extract some of the colour and flavour. Excessive extraction is avoided. The fermentation on skins is conducted for only a few days; then the mass of skins, pulp and partially fermented wine is transferred to the press. The mixture of free run and any pressings, if added, is transferred to a tank where it continues fermenting. It is normally only the free run and light pressings that are used in the production of tawny ports. When the fermentation reaches the desired sugar level the appropriate amount of spirit (alcohol) is added to increase the alcohol content to about 18% v/v. Sometimes brandy spirit is used in the fortification step, and some producers may add the spirit while the wine is still on skins. The addition of the spirit to 18% v/v stops the fermentation. The sugar levels of ports can be quite high; the actual level depends on the stage at which the fermentation is stopped by the addition of spirit, but it is normally well over 100, and often greater than 150, grams of sugar per litre. Wines that are fortified earlier in the fermentation contain more sugar.

After fortification the wine is clarified and transferred to old oak barrels and left to age for many years. The colour gradually changes from red to tawny brown. During this time the aromas and flavours also change and the wine takes on the characters that are derived from long ageing in barrels; they become more complex. Good tawny ports develop distinctive rancio characters. The flavours and acids become concentrated as water slowly evaporates through the barrels. The characters of the wine integrate over time, and the sweetness is balanced by the acids of the wine and the astringency of the oak extracted during the long period of oak storage. Many producers use a solera system to age their tawny ports, thus maintaining the consistency and quality of the style of wine they produce. At each bottling stage, wine is removed from the solera, blended, stabilised and bottled. Some of the components of the blend may be very old, especially in the more expensive wines.

Once a tawny port is bottled it is ready to be consumed. It does not need further ageing in the bottle; all its ageing has been carried out previously in oak barrels. When opened it should be consumed over a period of a few weeks, as after this time the wine in the partially filled bottle may loose its freshness.

Ruby port

Ruby Port is essentially a young tawny port. It has been aged for only a few years and will be ruby in colour, exhibiting a greater intensity of fruit type rather than aged characters.

SENSORY FEATURES OF TAWNY PORT

APPEARANCE

The colour is generally tawny brown. Older wines can show khaki and olive green tinges.

AROMAS AND FLAVOURS

The harmonious combination of aged wine, oak and spirit is the feature of these wines; usually words such as *nutty, walnuts, dried fruit, prune, coffee, caramel, toffee* and *rancio* are used to describe the characters. The older the wine, the greater the development of rancio characters. The spirit that has been added during the fortification can also add to the complexity of the bouquet and flavours. Some oak characters may also be present, such as vanillin.

The styles of tawny ports range from those with more youthful and fruity and less age emphasis, to the very complex styles that develop through long ageing.

THE PALATE

The palate, although sweet, should not be cloying. The sweetness should be balanced by the drying sensations that come from long ageing in oak barrels. The palate should be smooth and complex, with lingering flavours and a dry finish. The higher alcohol level may be obvious on the finish: a spicy, spirity, warming sensation at the back of the palate.

$\mathcal{V}$*intage port*

In Australia, vintage port is normally made from one or a combination of the varieties Shiraz, Cabernet Sauvignon, Grenache and Touriga. Grapes for this style of port should attain high sugar levels (about 14° Baumé) but must also have strong varietal aromas and flavours. They are fermented on skins to obtain maximum extraction of colour, tannin and flavour, and pressings are usually added to the free run. The wine is fortified when the desired sugar level is reached, spirit being added to raise the alcohol level to about 18% v/v. After completion of fermentation the wine is settled and stored separately until bottled. Because the wine is a vintage style it is not blended with any aged wine. The wine is normally stored in large oak barrels for one to two years and then bottled.

Vintage ports are made to develop for many years in the bottle, 10 to 20 years or more, before being consumed. These are normally only produced in years when the grapes ripen with all the right characters for extended ageing in the bottle. The wine is not necessarily stable or finely filtered when bottled and will normally throw a crust in the bottle. It requires careful decanting before being served.

Once opened the wine should be consumed in a few days, as the air in the partly filled bottle will modify the characters and the wine will loose its fresh, rich fruit characters.

SENSORY FEATURES OF VINTAGE PORT

APPEARANCE
The colour is normally ruby red. Young wines can be purple/black while older wines are light ruby red with some amber tones.

AROMAS AND FLAVOURS
These wines generally show rich, ripe berry fruit aromas and flavours. Words usually used to describe these wines include *violet, raspberry, black cherry, spice, blackberry, blackcurrant, plum, anise* and *licorice*, and depending on their age they may additionally show *chocolate, coffee, nutty* and *walnut* characters. They should not show any oak characters.

THE PALATE
Generally vintage port has a rich, full flavoured mid-palate and a firm, drying astringency from the tannins, leaving no lingering sweetness on the finish.

What you will see on the label
Tawny Port
These wines are labelled Tawny Port and/or have special names or codes. The label will often indicate the average age of the material used in preparing the blend.

Vintage Port
These wines are labelled Vintage Port and/or have special names or codes. The label indicates the year in which the wine was made.

The word port will eventually be removed from the labels of Australian wines of this style.

Some examples to try:

Traditionally these wine styles have been made by many producers in the Barossa, McLaren Vale, Riverland and north-eastern Victoria regions. Producers include:

Lindemans	Berri Estates	Seppelt
McWilliam's	Hardy	Angoves
Yalumba	Orlando	Peter Lehmann
Hardys	Chateau Yaldara	Penfolds
d'Arenberg	Wirra Wirra	Saltram
Kays	Brown Brothers	

and wineries in the Rutherglen area.

Some special tawny ports to try include:

Seppelt DP 90, Yalumba Galway Pipe, McWilliam's Hanwood, Saltram Mr Pickwick's and Penfolds Grandfather.

The range of vintage ports is not as great as that of tawny ports. Good examples come from Hardys, Brown Brothers, the wineries of the Rutherglen region and d'Arenberg from McLaren Vale.

Muscat and Tokay

Muscat is the luscious, fortified, sweet wine style made from very ripe Frontignac grapes. Tokay is a similar style of wine made from very ripe Muscadelle grapes.

The grape varieties

Frontignac

The official name for Frontignac is 'Muscat à Petit Grains', meaning Muscat with small berries. There are three forms, white, red and brown. Grapes from the various forms of Frontignac are used to make muscat style wines in a number of the warm to hot and hot grapegrowing regions of Australia, including the Barossa, the Riverland, Milawa and Corowa. But it is in the Rutherglen region in north-eastern Victoria that the brown form (Muscat à Petit Grains Rouge, known locally as Brown Muscat) produces Muscat of Rutherglen, a wine style unique in Australia and throughout the wine-producing world.

Muscadelle

The wine style tokay originates from a case of mistaken identity. The early vignerons of the Rutherglen region thought that particular vines growing in their region were the same variety that is used to make the famous tokai dessert wines in the Tokay-Hegyalja district of Hungary. They called these vines and the wines made from them tokay. However, in 1976 these vines were identified as the white grape variety Muscadelle. Although the true identity of these vines is now known, the wine continues to be called tokay.

How these wines are made

In the warm autumn climate the grapes ripen and shrivel (raisin) on the vines producing natural sugar levels in the range of 17 to 20° Baumé. In exceptional years this shrivelling effect produces raisined grapes which give a juice of about 25° Baumé.

The grapes are picked and crushed and yeast is added. Crushing produces a mixture of juice, skins, seeds and whole raisins. The sugar level of the juice may be in the order of 20° Baumé. The mixture is allowed to stand for a few days, extra sugar is leached from the raisins and the sugar level of the juice may increase to about 25° Baumé. During this time the yeast is slowly fermenting the sugar. Just as the sugar level starts to drop, spirit is added to increase the alcohol level to about 18% v/v and the fermentation ceases. Because the spirit is added so early in fermentation, these wines are very high in sugar, about 300 grams or more of sugar per litre. This contributes to their luscious tastes. But they are also complex. The fortified juice is stored and matured in large oak barrels (up to 2000 litres) for many years, gaining complexity as the components of the juice are slowly modified with time. The result is a luscious, complex, intensely flavoured wine. Many producers use a solera system to store their wines and some wines in these systems are many years older than the winemaker preparing the blend, the older wines having been laid down by their father or even their grandfather. These older wines are more complex and are often used in the very special blends prepared by the different producers.

What you will see on the label

These wines are labelled muscat and tokay. The word 'liqueur' loosely means that the wine is very sweet and luscious. It is somewhat confusing as other muscats and tokays without the word 'liqueur' are also very sweet and luscious. The word is used on labels of both young and old wines. The Muscat of Rutherglen winemakers are currently developing guidelines for a labelling system that will clearly indicate the different styles of muscat, eg, a system based on the age of the blending material and the sugar level of the wine. With time the use of terms 'liqueur' and old may be deleted.

A tasting experience

• Many producers made a range of products varying in the proportion of aged wine contained in the blend. The wines with a greater proportion of older wines are often the most expensive. An example is the range from Campbells:

Campbells Rutherglen Liqueur Muscat
average age 5 years.

Campbells Old Rutherglen Muscat
average age 12 years, some material 40 years old.

Campbells Merchant Prince Rutherglen Muscat
average age 25 years, some material 60 years old.

• For a very special occasion, indulge yourself with a memorable tasting experience with Chambers Old Liqueur Tokay.

SENSORY FEATURES OF MUSCAT AND TOKAY

APPEARANCE

These wines can range in colour from reddish gold with amber tinges through to tawny and deep browns with olive or khaki green hues. Swirl the wine in the glass and note how the wine slowly slides down the inside of the glass, leaving so-called tears or legs as the viscous liquid clings to the side.

BOUQUET AND FLAVOURS

The bouquet and flavours of these wines are rich, complex and entrancing.

Muscat

The distinctive character is *raisin* but also with *prune, toffee, caramel, butterscotch, nutty, walnut, dried fruit, fruitcake* and *rancio* characters.

Tokay

The distinctive character is *cold tea* but also with *fish oil, raisin, toffee, caramel, butterscotch, nutty, orange peel, dried fruit, fruitcake* and *rancio* characters.

THE PALATE

The palate should be fresh and with luscious, concentrated, complex, lingering flavours. Even though these wines have a high sugar content the sweet taste should be balanced by acid and oak components to give a dry finish. A warming sensation may be present at the back of the palate due to the higher alcohol content.

Tokay often seems to taste less sweet than muscat.

These wines are at their peak when bottled.

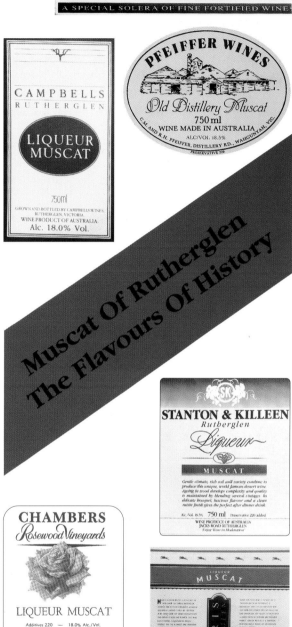

Muscat Of Rutherglen
The Flavours Of History

Enjoy muscat and tokay with sweet desserts, fruit cake, fresh fruit, cheese, nuts, dried fruits or after-dinner coffee.

Leasingham's Provis Vineyard near Clare.

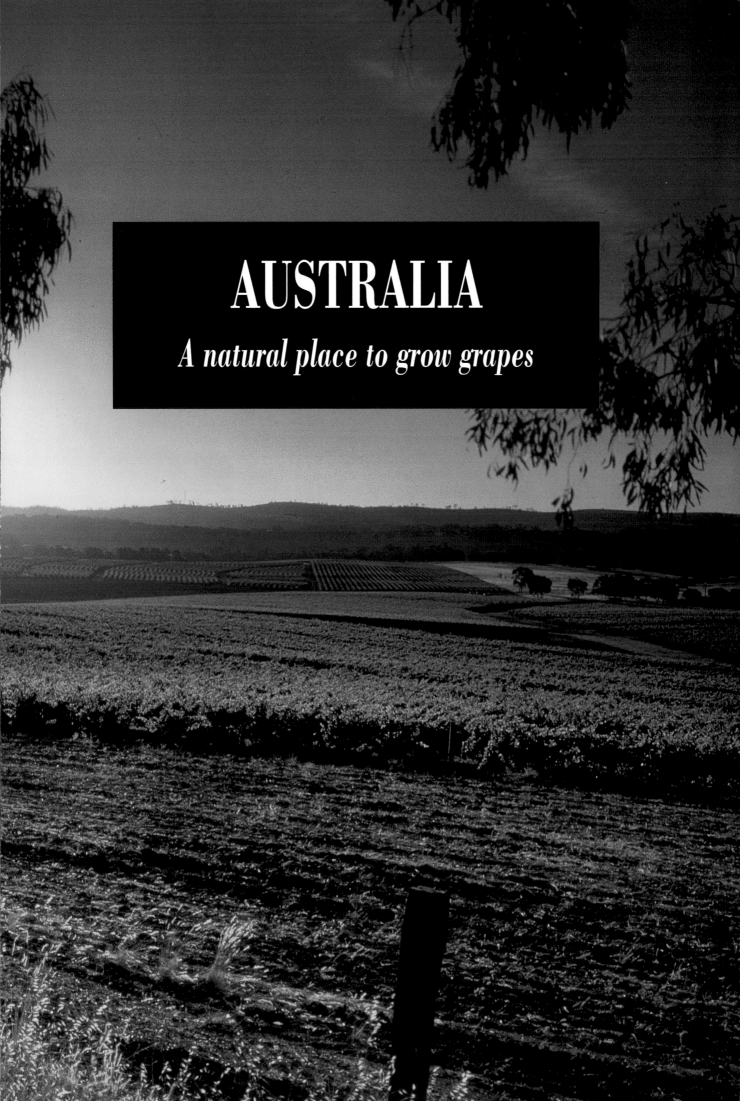

AUSTRALIA

A natural place to grow grapes

Climate, grapes and wine

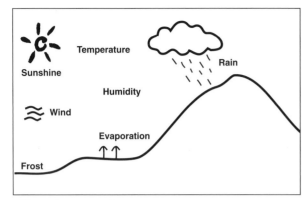

Climate has many elements.

Describing the climate of vinegrowing regions

All the climatic elements are important in grape production, however if emphasis were to be given to one it would be temperature. Temperature affects vine growth and berry composition, in some cases quite dramatically. Temperature also forms the basis for the various classification systems for describing vinegrowing regions. It is often the most obvious difference between sites.

Temperature

One approach to classifying vineyards according to their temperature characteristics is to categorise them in relation to the mean January temperature at that site.

This classification was developed by two Australian viticulturists, Dr Richard Smart and Mr Peter Dry. Although January does not correspond to the ripening period for most vineyard sites, the measure of the mean temperature for this month does broadly reflect the general climatic conditions during the ripening period in the different sites, and based on this index vineyards can be classified into very hot, hot, warm, cool or cold climatic sites, as described below.

A combination of terms

A combination of the climatic terms gives the best description of a particular vinegrowing region. For example the Rutherglen region in Victoria could be described as having a hot, very sunny, continental type of climate, while the climate of the Launceston region in Tasmania could be described as cool, moderately sunny, humid and moderately maritime.

If a region is described as having a *continental* climate, it means that there is generally a large difference between summer and winter temperatures. *Maritime* climates on the other hand show smaller fluctuation between summer and winter temperatures. Regions with continental climates are normally further inland, while regions categorised as maritime are near the coast or in close proximity to large bodies of water.

The warm to hot climates of the vineyards in the Rutherglen region are suitable for the production of full-bodied table wines from, eg, Chardonnay and Shiraz and some of the best sweet fortified wines in the world.

The cooler climates of the vineyards around Launceston are quite suited for the production of medium-bodied table wines from Riesling, Chardonnay and Pinot Noir.

Climatic description of site	Mean January temperature of site (°C)	
very hot	>23	
hot	21 - 22.9	There are no definite cut off points between classifications, but some arbitrary figures need to be set so that general groupings into the various climatic descriptions can be made.
warm	19 - 20.9	
cool	17 - 18.9	
cold	<16.9	

Heat summation index

Another climatic index that is frequently used in describing vineyard sites is *Heat Degree Days*. It is a heat summation index, ie, how much heat a particular vineyard site receives over the growing season. It is an alternative expression of the temperature conditions at that site. It is a more quantitative way of describing the temperature conditions of different vineyards. Various modifications of this index have been advanced by viticulturists over the years.

In this book we have chosen to use a modification of the heat degree day system termed *biologically effective day degrees*. This was developed by an Australian agricultural scientist, Mr John Gladstones; who was also involved in identifying many of the new vinegrowing areas in Western Australia. This index links temperature conditions of the site more closely with the biological activity of the vine and, as John Gladstones argues, it gives a better relationship with actual observations of vine growth and performance seen in the vineyard.

A general association exists between the words we use to describe the temperature conditions of a vineyard site and the biologically effective day degrees of that site. Vineyard sites classified descriptively as hot, normally have higher values for biologically effective day degrees, and so on. Because the terms evolve from different concepts it is not appropriate to define sharp cut-off points between the various gradations of the two systems; however the diagram on page 144 does give a guide to the relationship between the two expressions.

Yalumba's Oxford Landing Vineyard in the Riverland region of South Australia.

Delatite's vineyards in the foothills of the alps near Mansfield in the High Country region of Victoria.

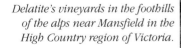

Australia's vineyards span the climatic spectrum

143

A general guide to the Heat summation index and climatic classification (vertical axis), Average % relative humidity (horizontal axis) and an estimate of the Average daily mean temperature during the ripening period (numbers in brackets) for some of Australia's vinegrowing regions

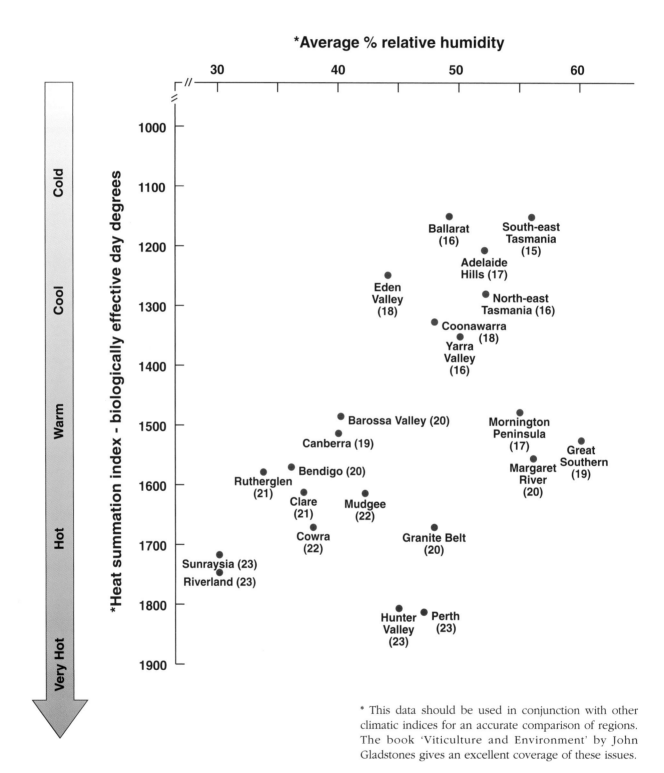

*Average % relative humidity

30 40 50 60

Heat summation index - biologically effective day degrees

Cold
Cool
Warm
Hot
Very Hot

1000
1100
1200
1300
1400
1500
1600
1700
1800
1900

Ballarat (16)
South-east Tasmania (15)
Adelaide Hills (17)
Eden Valley (18)
North-east Tasmania (16)
Coonawarra (18)
Yarra Valley (16)
Barossa Valley (20)
Canberra (19)
Mornington Peninsula (17)
Great Southern (19)
Bendigo (20)
Rutherglen (21)
Margaret River (20)
Clare (21)
Mudgee (22)
Cowra (22)
Granite Belt (20)
Sunraysia (23)
Riverland (23)
Hunter Valley (23)
Perth (23)

* This data should be used in conjunction with other climatic indices for an accurate comparison of regions. The book 'Viticulture and Environment' by John Gladstones gives an excellent coverage of these issues.

$\mathcal{S}$ome words of caution when interpreting the climatic classification

Variation within a region due to location

Temperature conditions may change over a very short range within a region. Individual vineyards within each region may not match the classification of the overall region, since they may be at a higher elevation and thus cooler than the climatic station where the temperature is recorded. For example, many sites within the general classification of Clare, in South Australia, are cooler than suggested by the data from the recording station, due to quite large differences among the vineyards in their altitudes, latitudes and individual topographics; thus justifying the description of the vineyards in the Clare region as ranging from cool, cool to warm and warm. Similar arguments apply to specific vineyards in other sites.

Other climatic factors can modify the effects of temperature

The temperature conditions during the ripening period are important in setting the balance between the sugar, acid, flavour and phenolic compounds of the berries.

However, other aspects such as wind, humidity, whether the vineyard is on a slope or in a valley, or near a large body of water may also modify the temperature conditions of individual vineyards.

Because of the influence of other climatic factors, temperature conditions can not always be taken as a direct indication of ripening conditions and potential wine style. For example, in the Hunter Valley the conditions are more suitable for ripening grapes for table wine styles than would initially be expected from observation of temperature conditions. It is likely that the higher humidity and sea breezes that occur in this region have an effect in relieving vine stress during ripening, providing more efficient ripening conditions.

Therefore, within each region it is important to know the particular conditions of any site in relation to the region as a whole.

Temperature conditions at any one site can vary from year to year: ***The vintage variation***

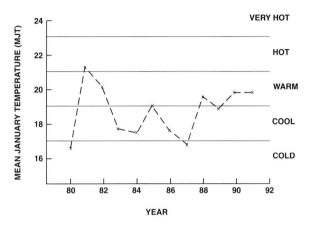

This illustration shows how the Mean January Temperature has changed over recent years for a vineyard sited in a cool region.

Because the climate of any region may vary from year to year, some vineyards will fluctuate from their classification each year, for example, a cool vineyard site may experience cold, cool or warm conditions during the period of grape development and ripening, depending on the climate of that year. Hence these regions have so-called 'great', 'good', and 'not so good' years.

Similarly, sites classified as warm fluctuate from cool to hot depending on the year. The wines will reflect the prevalent climatic conditions experienced up to and during the ripening period.

In hotter vinegrowing regions, although temperature does vary from year to year the temperature conditions generally remain hot. The climatic conditions during ripening are more consistent from year to year and thus there is usually less vintage variation in the wines produced from these regions.

Vineyard management practices can modify the effects of climate

Sound vineyard management practices are required to bring out the best in grapes from any climate. Practices that provide conditions which lead to vines with open canopies and which are adequately supplied with water and nutrients generally enhance grape composition. The vineyard management practices must be matched to the soil and climatic conditions of the site.

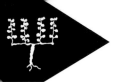

All grape varieties do not ripen at the same time

The cycle of vine growth occurs at different times of the year for different vineyard sites. Budburst and shoot growth commence in Spring, normally when the mean daily temperature reaches about 10°C, and thus these stages of vine growth occur first in hotter regions. As a rule these differences in growth pattern are carried through to harvest, for example budburst and shoot growth occur in the Barossa Valley (a warm to hot region) about mid-September and harvest takes place during March, while in a cool vineyard area, such as sites in Tasmania, budburst occurs about the beginning of October and harvest not until early to mid April.

However within each climatic region all grape varieties do not grow and ripen over the same time period. Grape varieties can be grouped into early, mid or late ripening varieties; at any one site the early ripening varieties are normally harvested earlier than varieties in the other groups.

Early ripening varieties include Pinot Noir and Chardonnay, while Shiraz and Riesling are classified as mid ripening varieties and Cabernet Sauvignon a mid to late ripening variety. Tarrango, a new red wine grape variety bred by researchers at the CSIRO laboratories at Merbein (Victoria), is a late ripening variety.

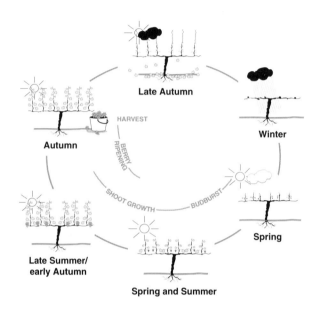

The annual cycle of vine growth.

A comparison of the times of ripening for some of the more well known grape varieties

In any one area these varieties are likely to be harvested first, signalling the start of vintage.

Early ripening	Mid-season ripening	Late ripening
Pinot Noir	Cabernet Sauvignon	Grenache
Chardonnay	Malbec	Tarrango
Sultana	Shiraz	Muscat Gordo Blanco
Traminer	Cabernet Franc	
Verdelho	Ruby Cabernet	*These varieties will be amongst the last to be harvested. The vintage for that year is almost over.*
	Chenin Blanc	
	Colombard	
	Crouchen	
	Marsanne	
	Riesling	
	Sauvignon Blanc	
	Semillon	

Matching the variety and the climate

Another difference between grape varieties is their ability to reach an adequate grape sugar level for the production of particular types of wine. This feature is linked with the concept of heat summation, some varieties having a lower heat summation requirement to attain the grape sugar level appropriate for making certain wine types. Mr John Gladstones categorises varieties into groups according to their biologically effective day degrees requirement to reach a certain level of sugar in the grapes. The example given below relates to a variety's heat summation requirement to attain a sugar level of about 12 °Baume (ie, a level suitable for the production of dry red or dry white table wine).

Variety	Heat summation requirement (biologically effective day degrees)
Pinot Noir	1150
Chardonnay	1150
Traminer	1150
Riesling	1200
Shiraz	1250
Cabernet Sauvignon	1300
Tarrango	1400

Varieties which require a larger heat summation to ripen fully are not suitable for cold and cold to cool sites. Grown in these cooler conditions these varieties will be ripening during a period (eg, April and May) when mean daily temperatures are falling as winter approaches. Varieties such as Cabernet Sauvignon may have difficulty in achieving good grape sugar levels for production of medium- to full-bodied dry red wine and, if adequate sugar is attained, the accompanying varietal aroma and flavour may often be dominated by capsicum type characters; a feature frequently associated with Cabernet Sauvignon grown in cooler climates. A variety such as Tarrango would have little chance of ripening fully in cool conditions as there would simply not be sufficient heat for its particular growth and ripening pattern. It was in fact developed specifically to match the ripening conditions occurring in hot areas and under these circumstances produces a light-bodied, well flavoured red wine with good natural acidity.

Varieties which require less heat to ripen, such as Chardonnay, Traminer, Riesling and Pinot Noir, will ripen adequately in cool, warm or hot regions but they produce a different style of wine in each climatic region.

In cold, cool and cool to warm climatic regions the vineyards are planted predominately with the varieties Pinot Noir, Chardonnay, Traminer and Riesling. Often, and particularly in the cooler regions, Pinot Noir and Chardonnay will be used to make sparkling wine. In warm and warm to hot, and hot regions we are more likely to find plantings of Cabernet Sauvignon, Shiraz, Grenache, Muscat Gordo Blanco and Frontignac as well as Chardonnay. Chardonnay appears to be a very adaptable grape variety and produces well flavoured wines (but of different styles) right across the climatic spectrum. Chardonnay is grown in many Australian regions and consequently we see many styles of Chardonnay wines.

Temperature: how it influences wine type

Temperature affects the photosynthetic process in the leaves since the function of the enzymes involved in sugar production is temperature sensitive. Enzymes are chemical substances that cause reactions in living cells to go faster. These sugar enzymes work best at between about 18 and 33°C. If the leaf temperature is either cold or extremely hot, production of sugar in the leaves is slowed and subsequent accumulation in the berries may be low and inappropriate for the production of certain wine types. Overall most sites classified as very hot, hot, warm or cool have sufficient periods (photosynthetic hours) during each day of the ripening period to satisfy this temperature requirement and almost always produce grapes with sugar levels appropriate for the production of most wine types.

However, in cold and cold to cool sites where daily temperatures are lower, particularly towards the end of ripening, there may be insufficient hours of this necessary temperature range to produce adequate amounts of sugar in the leaves and thus in the berries. In Australia these regions would include some of the more southerly and/or higher altitude vineyard sites (areas with low values for biologically effective day degrees). Delicate, light-bodied dry whites and sparkling wines are often produced from grapes grown in these regions, since these wine styles are made from grapes with lower sugar levels.

Grapes grown in cool to warm, warm and warm to hot regions normally reach adequate sugar levels for the production of medium- to full-bodied white and red table wines. Warm to hot and hot regions are often suited to growing grapes for the production of full-bodied white and red table wines as well as for fortified wines. Under these conditions there is a greater chance of attaining the higher sugar levels (between 16 and 20° Baumé) required for the production of fortified wines.

VERY HOT	
HOT	Fortified wines Full-bodied dry white and red wines
WARM	
	Medium-bodied dry white and red wines
COOL	Delicate dry white wines
COLD	Sparkling wines

A general relationship between temperature conditions of the vineyard site and the likely types/styles of wine that will be produced.

Temperature: creating characters of wine style

As well as influencing sugar accumulation in grapes, temperature also regulates the amounts and types of acid, colour, tannins and aroma and flavour compounds that develop in grapes during ripening. It thus has a controlling role in determining the style of wine produced from those grapes: how crisp the wine is on the palate (the acidity component), how the wine smells and tastes (the aroma and flavour component) and for red wines, how red coloured the wine will be (the colour component) and how the wine feels in the mouth (the tannin component).

Acidity

During berry ripening, the overall decrease in juice acidity level is partly due to the breakdown of malic acid, a process also controlled by enzymes. As a rule the higher the temperature the greater the loss (breakdown) of malic acid. Grapes from vineyards in warm to hot climates will on average have lower natural levels of acid than grapes from cooler conditions and may require acid adjustment prior to winemaking. Cool climates normally produce grapes which contain higher amounts of acid and the resultant wines will be more naturally acidic and fresher.

Colour

Production of colour (compounds called *anthocyanins*) occurs in the skin of black grapes; again modified by specific enzyme activity. These colour enzymes work best between 17 and 26°C. This range is somewhat lower than that for photosynthetic reactions and thus, while most grape-growing regions have temperature profiles that fulfil the temperature requirement for sugar production, some very hot regions will not be optimal for grape colour production. The temperature during a large part of the day in these sites will be too high for colour production, although adequate amounts of sugar may be obtained. In cold regions both sugar and colour production may be limited by the low temperature conditions. Thus, black grapes from vineyards in different climatic regions, may ripen to similar sugar levels, but the accompanying colour in the grapes may vary widely. The wines produced from those grapes will also be different; although of similar type (eg, dry red table wine) they could range in sensory characters from lightly coloured and light-bodied to highly coloured and full-bodied wines, ie, they will be of different styles.

Aroma and flavour

Temperature also regulates the production of aroma and flavour compounds in grapes. As yet we do not know the optimum temperature range for the enzymes involved in varietal aroma and flavour production, although it is likely to be similar to or slightly lower than that for colour production.

Experience does give us some clues as to the type of primary fruit characters to expect from grapes and wines from diverse temperature conditions. Each variety responds uniquely. Shiraz wines from cooler climates often display distinctive primary fruit characters described as spicy and peppery, while those from warmer regions may express more plum and mulberry-like aromas and flavours. Cooler growing conditions highlight the floral, fragrant aromas and flavours of Riesling grapes (and wines) while cool to warm and warm sites bring out more lime-like characters. The primary fruit characters of Chardonnay wines generally range through apple, lime, gooseberry, melon, rockmelon, peach, fig, fruit salad, to tropical fruit-like sensations as we progress from cool to hot vineyard sites.

The changes do not occur in distinct steps and for any situation there is an overlap of sensations. Most often it is groups of characters that are associated with specific climatic sites.

Wine style

Wine style is not just influenced by the temperature conditions in which the grapes grow; many other factors of climate, vine management and winemaking technique also play a role in influencing the make up of grapes and the taste of the wine. However, the effects of temperature produce a range of combinations of sugar, acid, colour and aroma and flavour compounds in grapes, which when carried over into the wine create different wine styles for each variety, ie, wines of varying alcoholic strength, acidity and smell and taste sensations. The following comments on the effects of temperature on wine style are given as a general guide to the types and styles of wine to expect from different climatic region. *These comments assume that the vines are grown according to sound management practices.*

The most suitable grapes for premium sparkling wine production come from Chardonnay and Pinot Noir vines grown in cold to cool climatic sites. Under these conditions they produce a high intensity of the right aromas and flavours at the lower sugar levels required for the production of these wines.

Medium-bodied white table wines (for example, Rieslings, Traminers, Chardonnays and Sauvignon Blancs) are normally produced from grapes grown in cool and cool to warm conditions. Their sensory characters will be described by terms more towards the earlier to mid stages of the primary fruit spectrum. Their natural acidity is frequently high, reflected by a crispness on the palate.

Cool to warm, warm, and warm to hot climatic conditions appear to be most suited to the production of medium- to full-bodied white and red table wines, such as Chardonnay, Pinot Noir, Cabernet Sauvignon and Shiraz. A range of rich but distinct aroma and flavour profiles may be evident, those in the middle and towards the later stage of the primary fruit spectrum. These wines can often have not only rich primary and developed fruit characters, but will also show great complexity and mouthfeel sensation. Red wines generally show good tannin structure. Alcohol levels of these wines are often around 12-14% v/v.

Grapes grown in hotter climates often, but not always, produce medium- to full-bodied wines of lesser dimensions of aroma and flavour sensations, and of medium intensity of colour and overall aroma and flavour. Palate structure of the wine produced in such conditions may not be as good as that of wines from warm conditions. Acidity adjustment is normally required prior to winemaking.

Warm to hot and hot conditions are also suited to the production of fortified wine styles, in this case higher sugar levels, as well as intensity of flavours, being an important requirement.

The flavour spectrums for the different grape varieties are described in the relevant sections on wine styles.

Temperature: only part of the climate story

Although a critical aspect in setting wine style, temperature is only part of the complex array of events that influence grape composition and wine style. The effects of other climatic elements such as sunshine hours, humidity, rainfall, evaporation and wind on vine growth and grape ripening need to be considered before deciding on any particular site for growing grapes.

Sunshine

Sunshine provides the energy for photosynthesis. Most Australian vine-growing regions have sufficient sunshine hours during the growing season to provide adequate ripening conditions. Many of our vineyard sites are aptly described as sunny and warm, conditions that are conducive to producing not only well flavoured grapes with adequate sugar levels, but also grapes that are free of disease and in sound condition at harvest.

However, it is not only leaves that benefit from sun exposure; grape berries also require light to initiate reactions that lead to colour, aroma and flavour development. For vineyards in cool and warm climatic sites the more the bunches are exposed to sunlight, generally the greater production of colour and aroma and flavour compounds in the berries. However, exposure, as well as increasing light interception, may also raise the temperature of the berry; in hotter environments this may be detrimental to the reactions causing colour, aroma and flavour development. Thus in hot climates some but not total bunch exposure may be the best option. Viticulturists need to set their management practices to complement the effects of the environment.

Sunshine within the vine canopy.

Humidity and evaporation

Sites that have high evaporation and low humidity are associated with higher transpiration rates (ie, water loss through the leaves). Irrigation may be necessary to maintain efficient leaf function in order to prevent the vines becoming stressed during critical growth periods. Water is essential to the functioning of the vine and many Australian vineyards benefit from regulated irrigation, improving grape and wine quality.

Environments with lower evaporation and higher humidity are more favourable for avoiding vine moisture stress; however such environments are often associated with higher rainfall during the growing season, which can lead to a higher incidence of fungal diseases. In these sites good vine management practices are required to provide sound grapes for winemaking.

Wind

Some wind may be beneficial to vines; it can dry out the leaves after rain and help prevent the onset of disease. On the other hand, very windy sites can impair vine growth, and vineyards in such environments are often protected by wind breaks.

Site selection

The effects of all these climatic elements guide the viticulturist in selecting an appropriate vineyard site. The first decision, though, must be: 'What type/style of wine is to be produced?' Selecting a site with the appropriate temperature conditions for that type/style of wine is the next step. Within the selected site the best position is then chosen in relation to soil type and other climatic considerations such as protection from wind and frost.

The methods employed in selecting new vineyard sites now involve extensive surveys of climate, soil and water resources and consideration of the most appropriate varieties to match the climatic conditions.

Modern technology and management practices are employed in the construction and maintenance of these sites, as typified in the establishment of Richmond Grove Vineyard at Cowra, New South Wales.

**FROM
THIS**

*T*he establishment of Richmond Grove's Vineyard at Cowra.

Vine rows were set up using laser technology to ensure that the vine rows were straight so that pruning and harvesting operations can be fully mechanised. Irrigation is applied automatically by a centralised, computer-driven irrigation system.

The established trellis system where modern canopy management techniques are used to ensure open canopies such as:

**TO
THIS**

The Scott Henry trellis system.

Now planted with a range of premium wine grape varieties.

151

$\mathcal{M}$anaging the vine

Microclimate

Climate and other environmental influences are only part of the wine style equation. How the vine is managed also plays a part in the development and ripening of the grapes and the completion of the ripening equation.

Leaves and fruit require sunlight, and the arrangement of the shoots should enable as much sunlight as possible to penetrate the canopy. Small vines with spacious canopies achieve this naturally, while for other situations human intervention is needed to order the vine's shape through trellising. A great variety of trellis systems has been developed, particularly in the last few decades, and this area has evolved its own jargon: G.D.C. (Geneva Double Curtain), V.S.P. (Vertical Shoot Positioned), Scott Henry, and Lyre, to give a few examples.

Essentially these trellis systems all serve the same purpose: to arrange the shoots of the vine in such a way that the leaves and fruit receive optimal sunlight in that particular site. Vines that are grown on shallow or poor soils normally require simple trellis systems, while those grown on rich, deep soils usually require more elaborate trellis systems. Viticulturists refer to this as getting the microclimate right. The right microclimate enhances the biological activity of leaves and fruit and adds to, rather than detracts from, the desired grape composition. Grapes from open canopies, as a rule, have improved sugar accumulation and sugar/acid balance, increased grape colour and more desirable primary fruit characters.

Viticulturists have found that they can modify wine style through canopy management. For example, some wines made from the variety Cabernet Sauvignon can have a dominant capsicum- like smell and taste, a feature originating in the grapes and very often associated with grapes coming from cooler growing conditions and/or from shaded canopies. The intensity of this character in the grapes can be decreased by changing the trellis system so that leaves and bunches are more exposed to light. The changes in the primary fruit spectrum of the grapes lead to a refinement of the style of the wine coming from those grapes.

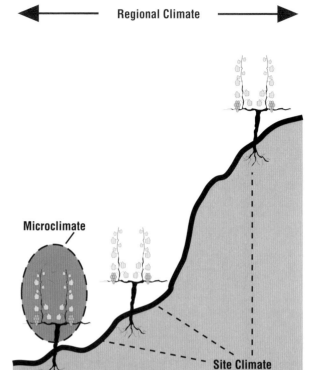

Climate can be defined in different ways.

Some definitions of climate:

- *Regional climate* - the climatic conditions that apply to a particular region.
- *Site climate* - the climatic conditions that apply to a particular site within a region.
- *Microclimate* - the climatic condition around and within the canopy, in the immediate vicinity of the leaves and bunches.

Similarly the primary fruit spectrum of other varieties can be manipulated in the vineyard. Another example is the fine-tuning of the amount of asparagus-like character in Sauvignon Blanc grapes. Greater exposure of leaves and bunches to light can lessen the intensity of the asparagus-like character while increasing gooseberry and tropical fruit-like characters.

In addition to selecting the right trellis, other cultural practices may be required to enhance fruit quality. Leaves may be removed in the vicinity of the bunches to ensure maximum sunlight interception, a practice that can increase grape colour as well as modifying fruit flavours. Special machines have been developed to carry out this operation, although in many vineyards it is still done manually.

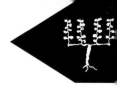

*T*rellis systems provide support for the growth of the vine, arranging the shoots of the vine (the canopy) in such a way that the leaves and fruit receive optimal sunlight for any particular site. You will hear vinegrowers talk about the different ways that they manage the canopies of their vines in order to get *'the microclimate right.'*

Some options in canopy management ....

Not all vines require a trellis system. These bush vines in the Barossa Valley are small enough to support themselves.

Some vines will only need a simple trellis system where a single wire is erected along the row to hold the arms of the vine and its foliage off the ground. The spiky nature of the canopy allows sunlight to penetrate into the interior of the canopy.

Vertical shoot positioning: a system where all the shoots are trained upwards through foliage wires.

The Scott-Henry system: In some sites positioning all the shoots upwards may cause crowding and shading within the canopy. A Scott-Henry trellis system can be used, where half the number of shoots for any section of the row are positioned upwards and the other half downwards.

The Lyre system: Canopies can also be divided horizontally to form two sections which are positioned upwards.

Geneva Double Curtain (GDC) system: Canopies can also be divided and positioned downwards.

Yield

This is commonly referred to as the weight of grapes per area of vineyard and is expressed as tonnes per hectare or tonnes per acre.

One tonne per acre is equivalent to 2.5 tonnes per hectare.

Yields of Australian vineyards range from about 3 to about 40 tonnes/hectare, depending on the variety, site and associated vineyard practices. There is no magical figure for the optimum yield at any one site. It depends on the style of wine that the winemaker wishes to produce, and relates to establishing conditions which provide adequate active leaf area to ripen the amount of grapes on each vine for that style of wine (both *sugar ripe* and *flavour ripe*). These conditions will vary with variety, site and desired wine style.

In the main, wines that are highly regarded as benchmarks for their style of wine are produced from lower rather than higher yielding vineyards. Wines showing great structure and intensity of flavours are, as a rule, produced from well managed vineyards yielding less than 10 tonnes per hectare and frequently lower than 5 tonnes per hectare. However any specific relationship must be judged with caution, as assessment on yield alone ignores the other aspect of vine management. With sound vine management, vineyards yielding in excess of 10 tonnes per hectare can produce excellent wines. Each particular situation must be judged on its merits, and ultimately rests with the quality of the finished wine in the glass.

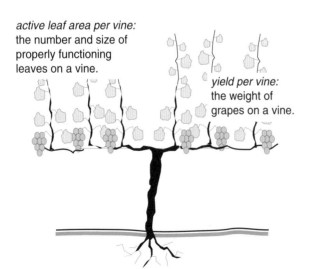

active leaf area per vine: the number and size of properly functioning leaves on a vine.

yield per vine: the weight of grapes on a vine.

There may be one, two or three bunches of grapes and anywhere from ten to thirty leaves on a shoot, and many combinations of numbers of leaves and bunches can occur in different situations. However, it is the overall ratio of active leaf area to the weight of grapes that appears to be crucial. Within limits, quality grapes may be produced from vines which have short shoots and small bunches or from vines with longer shoots and larger bunches.

If the ratio is very low (too few active leaves or too high a weight of grapes) accumulation of sugar in the berries may be slowed and the fruit may not be sugar ripe at harvest for particular wine types, a circumstance referred to as *overcropping*. Accompanying levels of grape colour, aroma and flavour will also be low. Overcropping may occur in very cool sites where low temperatures may limit leaf activity, in situations where leaf function is hindered by water stress or shaded canopy conditions, and/or where yield is excessively high. Simply put, there is not enough sugar to be shared amongst the berries on the vine.

In well-managed vineyards, overcropping is normally not a problem, and most vineyards will produce fruit that is of the required sugar level for the desired wine type. However, this ratio of active leaves to the weight of the grapes also influences the amount of colour and the intensity and types of aroma and flavour compounds in the berries, since the reactions forming these require a supply of sugar. For any one variety, changing this ratio may also modify the style of the wine coming from those vines. Up to a point, the higher the ratio, the more sugar is available, and in these conditions grapes with similar sugar levels will have higher berry colour as well as a greater intensity of primary fruit characters. Again, simply put, there is more sugar to go around and so there are more aroma and flavour compounds produced in the berries.

The ratio can be improved by manipulating the vine either to increase the leaf area or to decrease the weight of grapes.

Many vineyards are now fitted with trellis extensions so that another trellis wire can be fitted to hold the shoots upright, allowing them to grow longer and bear more leaves before they need to

be trimmed during summer. But it is not just a matter of having more leaves; these leaves must be functioning efficiently, and for this to happen they must be well exposed to light, free of disease and supplied with adequate nutrients and water.

Some growers will cut bunches off (*bunch thinning*) at about veraison. This reduces the overall weight of grapes on the vine and in certain situations can improve not only sugar accumulation but also the development of colour and flavour of the grapes on the remaining bunches.

Irrigation

> *Irrigation - crucial to optimal vine performance in many Australian vineyards.*

Many Australian vineyards are sited in environments with winter dominant rainfall and high evaporation during the summer months, conditions which can lead to depletion of soil moisture during the growth and ripening of the vine. Under such conditions it is critical that additional water be supplied to the vine by irrigation, relieving vine stress and improving vine performance overall. On the other hand, too much irrigation or rain during the ripening period can swell the berries and dilute the concentration of sugar and other berry components. Controlled irrigation is the best approach and modern vineyards are now irrigated so that different sections of the vineyard receive different amounts of water, depending on the soil type in that section.

Pruning

Pruning is an annual event normally carried out in winter, in which parts of the dormant shoots are cut off the vine. Traditionally it has been done by hand, but now it is more common to prune with the aid of various forms of machines. Machine pruning (also called mechanical pruning) reduces the time and high cost involved in hand pruning.

In some cases vines are essentially not pruned at all. This concept of minimal pruning, in which only shoots hanging close to the ground are trimmed (either in winter or summer), was developed in Australia and has proved to be successful in many vinegrowing regions. Minimally pruned vines have many more shoots and smaller bunches per vine and generally are higher yielding than conventionally pruned vines. The shoots are short and grow on the outside of the canopy, providing good leaf and bunch exposure. Berries are small, a feature which results in a concentration of sugar and other berry components.

It has been convincingly demonstrated that well-managed mechanically and minimally pruned vines, as well as having cost advantages in grape production, can produce consistently good wines. Many highly regarded red and white table wines have their origins in vineyards using these techniques or modifications of them.

You will find that in any one vinegrowing region some growers will manually cane prune or spur prune their vines, while others will machine prune. Via experience, each chooses to use a system that gives the best grapes for the desired style of wine.

Wines that command high prices can justify extra work in the vineyard, such as hand pruning and other costly vineyard practices, while wines that are sold at lower price points require application of cultural practices in the vineyard that are highly mechanized. Mechanical pruning and machine harvesting are now widely accepted practices in Australian viticulture. Adoption of these practices has been significant in producing well flavoured wines at reasonable prices.

Disease control

Most Australian vineyards are located in climates that are sunny and dry during the period of vine growth and grape ripening, conditions that are ideal for growing healthy, disease free grapes. In sites where rainfall or humidity during the growing season is higher, there will be a greater incidence of fungal disease. The incidence and intensity of these diseases is much less in open canopies where air movement can dry out the leaves and bunches. Integrating pruning and trellis systems to achieve open canopies can minimise the need for chemical sprays in preventing these diseases. Viticulturists, not only in Australia but world wide, are mindful of the environment and are moving towards management systems that will allow them to produce grapes with low, or in some cases, no chemical input. Luckily, in Australia the climate of many of our vineyards is favourable to such an approach.

Hand pruning vines at Mitchelton winery, Victoria.

A cane pruned vine.

Mechanically pruning vines.

Spur pruned vines. The vines in the background are still to be pruned.

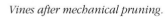

Vines after mechanical pruning.

Minimally pruned vines.

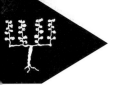

The soil

The soil: where it all begins.

The soil provides anchorage for the vine and acts as a source of nutrients and water which are taken up by the vine roots. Grapevines will grow in a wide range of soil types; often the most limiting factor is availability of soil water, although this can normally be provided through irrigation. In general, suitable soils are those that have sufficient depth and are well-aerated, well-drained and have good water holding capacity. A range of soil types from sandy loams through to loam clays provide these conditions. Nutrient deficiencies, if any, can be supplied through the application of fertilisers.

Some soils do seem to have special properties, a topic we discuss next under the heading of terroir. One such soil in Australia is red earth over limestone; commonly called *Terra Rossa*. These soils are found in a number of Australia's grape-growing regions. It is generally regarded as providing the character of the great wines of the Coonawarra district of South Australia. Whether it has some magical properties or whether the important fact is that it is very well drained compared to the neighbouring black soil, and/or that vines on the Terra Rossa soils have more favourable microclimates, remains debatable....

Terroir

Any association between specific soil types and wine quality is an issue that remains to be resolved. Certainly there is an indirect effect in that soil type influences the growth and function of the vine, altering the canopy microclimate, the yield and the ripening process. These changes often have a dramatic effect on grape composition and the style of the wine made from those grapes. This complex link between the soil and the taste of wine is incorporated in the meaning of the French word *terroir*. However, the term terroir really deals with the combined effects of the interaction of the vine with its soil and its climate. In other words, the influence of the vine's micro-environment on its performance and ripening pattern.

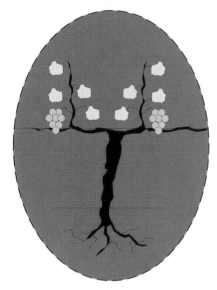

Terroir: the micro-environment in which the vine grows.

Yet the word micro-environment, which encompasses the interrelated effects of soil and canopy, does not conjure up the same emotions and images as does the word terroir. Vineyard practices which influence the vine's micro-environment have often evolved from hundreds of years experience in growing vines and making wines in one particular region. Thus in the traditional wine regions of Europe the term terroir also encompasses the viticultural practices associated with that particular region and its people.

Every vineyard has its terroir. It is just that some vineyards have special terroirs, ones that consistently produce great wines. The interaction of the vine with its climate and its soil is such that, as yet, we do not know if there is some magical mix of soil components that gives these vineyard sites some special advantage in the way they ripen their grapes. An element of the unknown does add to the anticipation, atmosphere and enjoyment associated with tasting these special wines.

The famous Coonawarra 'Terra Rossa' soil and some of the wines that come from it.

Getting it right in the vineyard

Climate can have a dramatic effect on the growth of vines, the composition of grapes, wine type and style. We have discussed many of these effects throughout this chapter.

Superimpose the effects of soil and vine management onto those of climate, and you can well imagine the many possible combinations of sugar, acid, colour and aroma and flavour compounds that can develop in grapes in different ripening situations.

Soil may vary in its depth and its proportions of sand, clay, limestone, rocks etc, even over short distances. Pruning, trellising, irrigation and other cultural practices will vary to match these changing conditions. These variations may occur from one vineyard to the next or even within sections of one vineyard. It follows then that grapes grown in similar climates but on different soils and/or with different management practices can achieve the same stage of ripeness in terms of sugar content but may have entirely different amounts of acid, colour and expressions of aromas and flavours; differences that are carried over into the wine.

Wines, made from the same variety grown in vineyards of similar climate, differ due to the variation in soil type and management practices of each vineyard.

Wines, made from the same variety but grown in vineyards with different climates, differ due to the variations in climate, soil type and management practices of each vineyard.

Ripeness has many definitions, each closely linked to a particular wine style. Simply put, it is when the grapes have the right amount of sugar, acid and colour and the right types of flavours for a particular wine style. *Ultimate ripeness* occurs when the combined effects of climate, soil and management practices are fine-tuned in such a way that the components of the grape evolve completely and perfectly for the production and development of wines that epitomise that style. This is a ripeness that, with time, provides a wine that gives ultimate tasting enjoyment, this being the prime purpose of wine.

Managing vineyards to achieve a desired grape composition for particular wine styles requires an integrated approach for each vineyard. The pruning method, the irrigation level, the trellis system and other viticultural practices all need to be matched to achieve the best from any one site. Sometimes this will be through traditional and well established practices; in other cases it will be achieved through innovative technology. It is all about nurturing the vine in such a way that it readily captures the available sunlight and then uses it to its fullest.

Climate and soil affect vine growth and grape composition.

*G*rape variety and vine management must be matched to the climatic and soil conditions of the vineyard.

Vine management affects vine performance and grape composition.

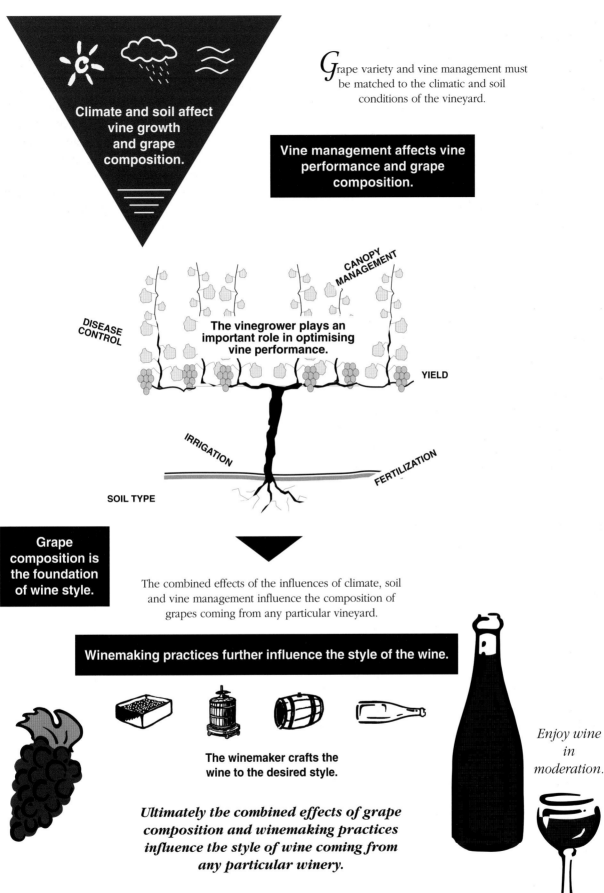

CANOPY MANAGEMENT

DISEASE CONTROL

The vinegrower plays an important role in optimising vine performance.

YIELD

IRRIGATION

FERTILIZATION

SOIL TYPE

Grape composition is the foundation of wine style.

The combined effects of the influences of climate, soil and vine management influence the composition of grapes coming from any particular vineyard.

Winemaking practices further influence the style of the wine.

The winemaker crafts the wine to the desired style.

Enjoy wine in moderation.

Ultimately the combined effects of grape composition and winemaking practices influence the style of wine coming from any particular winery.

It is now widely acknowledged that the varied natural conditions present throughout Australia are highly favourable to the growing of vines of a range of grape varieties; producing grapes which in due course our winemakers craft into the many styles of Australian wine.

Photographic acknowledgements

Photographs that refer to wineries, vineyards and/or bottles of wine, and where the associated wine company is mentioned in the photograph or in the caption, were provided by the respective wine companies.

Other photographs were provided as shown below:

A vineyard showing the effect of phylloxera (p32) by Greg Buchanan of The Victorian Department of Agriculture.

Machine harvesting (p43) by Gordon Lonnon of Gregoire.

Oak trees and barrel making (p49) by Geoff Schahinger of C.A. Schahinger.

Vinimatic rotary fermenter (p50) by John Sitters of The University of Adelaide.

Cork trees & corks (p53) and back cover by Bruce Priestley of J.B. Macmahon Pty Ltd.

Botrytised juice oozing from the press (p100) by Southcorp.

Botrytised grapes (p100) by Les Worland of De Bortoli Wines.

Barrels at the 12 o'clock and the 2 o'clock position (p114) and the barrel of flor sherry (p134) by John Kleinig of Southcorp.

Leconfield wine and food (p119 and inside back cover) was taken by Cliff Dykes Photography.

Food and wine (p139) by The Muscat of Rutherglen Association.

The G.D.C. trellis (p153) by Peter Dry of The University of Adelaide.

The profile of Coonawarra soil (p159) by Katnook Estate.

Photographs on p16,23 (vineyard and time), 26 (Katnook Estate and Chapel Hill), 43 (shiraz grapes), 153 (vineyard at top/right) were supplied by the South Australian Tourism Commission.

Photographs of wine bottles (p7,8,12,52), glasses of wine (p14,15,18,52,100,108), grapes with and without skins (p36), sparkling wine corks (p64) and wine labels were taken by Stan Richards Photography, Adelaide.

Other photography by Patrick Iland.

References

Anonymous. (1994) The Rewards of Patience (3rd Edition). Penfolds Wines Pty Ltd. Nuriootpa, South Australia, Australia.

Coombe, B.G. and Dry, P.R. (1988) Viticulture, Volume 1 Resources. Winetitles, Adelaide, South Australia, Australia.

Gladstones, J. (1992) Viticulture and Environment. Winetitles, Adelaide, South Australia, Australia.

Halliday, J. (1992) An Introduction to Australian Wine. Collins, Angus & Robertson (A division of Harper Collins) Pymble, New South Wales, Australia.

Norrie, P. (1994) Wine and Health Booklet. Available from McWilliam's Wines Pty Ltd, New South Wales, Australia.

$\mathscr{A}$ useful index